MOTORCYCLE CHRONICLE

ONE HUNDRED YEARS OF MAGNIFICENT MACHINES

BY DOUG MITCHEL

Publications International, Ltd.

Louis Weber, CEO
Publications International, Ltd.
7373 North Cicero Avenue
Lincolnwood, Illinois 60712

Permission is never granted for commercial purposes.

Manufactured in China.

8 7 6 5 4 3 2 1

ISBN: 0-7853-3350-9

Library of Congress Catalog Card Number: 00-110530

Photography

All photos by **Doug Mitchel**, except pages 214 and 215, contributed by **David Gooley**.

Owners

Thanks to the owners of the motorcycles featured for their enthusiastic cooperation. They are listed below, along with the page number(s) on which their bikes appear.

Dennis Ahrens, 290, 291; **Michael Aldrich**, 218, 219; **American Classics Museum**, 106; **Jim Anderson**, 100, 101; **Larry Anderson**, 96, 97, 294, 295; **John Archacki**, 104, 105, 116, 117, 144, 145; **Tom Baer**, 12, 13, 52, 53; **Banzai Motor Sports**, 300, 301, 304, 305, 310, 311; **Rex Barrett**, 244, 245, 252, 253; **Bob Baumgartner**, 98, 99, 140, 141; **Rick Bernard**, 228, 229; **Pete Bollenbach**, 10, 11, 14, 15, 30, 31, 42, 43, 50, 51, 56, 57, 72, 73, 78, 79, 80, 192, 193, 220, 221, 282, 283, 288, 289; **Marvin Bredemeir**, 92, 93; **Bud Burnett**, 129; **Don Chasteen**, 114, 115; **Vance Clute**, 81; **Dick Cogswell**, 166, 167, 182, 183; **E. J. Cole**, 34, 35; **Walter E. Cunny**, 86, 87; **Dale's Harley-Davidson**, 308, 309; **Dale Walksler's Wheels Through Time Museum**, 26, 27, 60, 61, 62, 63, 77, 89, 107, 241; **Ralph and Nancy Dam**, 124, 125; **Tom Eiden**, 172, 173; **Elgin Police Dept.**, 216, 217; **Dale Evans**, 230, 231; **Ben Frame**, 154, 155; **Dennis French**, 260, 261; **Jim Goebel**, 212, 213; **Hugh Hall**, 94, 95; **Henry Hardin Family**, 22, 23, 24, 25, 74; **Heritage Harley-Davidson**, 284, 285, 286, 287, 306, 307, 308, 309; **Martin Horn**, 148, 149, 250, 251; **Illinois Harley-Davidson**, 280, 281; **Lakeshore Harley-Davidson**, 256, 257; **Laurel BMW Motorcycles**, 278, 279; **Matt Jonas**, 164, 165, 178, 179, 194, 195, 224, 225, 234, 235, 248, 249, 258, 259, 264, 265; **Matt Kallas**, 246, 247; **John Kasper**, 254, 255; **Jim Kersting Family Collection**, 46, 47, 58, 59, 75, 122, 123, 136, 137, 168, 169, 222, 223; **Dave Kiesow, Illinois Harley-Davidson**, 68, 69, 89, 147, 240, 241; **David Kincaid**, 132, 133; **Kokesh Motorcycles**, 84, 85; **Steve and Lori Krings**, 298, 299; **Steve Kuscsik**, 238, 239; **Ray Landy**, 156, 157, 190, 191; **Matt Lane**, 316, 317; **John Lawton**, 268, 269; **Barbara Liles and Warren Dorn**, 204, 205; **Lee Mattes, Heritage Harley-Davidson**, 276, 277; **Bob Maxant, Illinois Harley-Davidson**, 36, 37; **R. B. McClean**, 18, 19, 28, 29, 112, 113, 126, 127, 186, 187; **Michael Mini**, 236, 237; **Jim, Jeff, and Kevin Minnis**, 110, 111, 128, 135, 142, 143, 196, 197, 198, 199; **Paul A. Misic**, 270, 271; **Steve Mitleider**, 262, 263; **David Monahan**, 88, 89; **Ted Moran**, 130, 131, 210, 211, 266, 267; **Jan Morgan**, 214, 215; **Motorcycle Center**, 272, 273, 292, 293, 312, 313, 314, 315; **John Murphy**, 102, 103, 120, 121; **John Olberg**, 40, 41; **Otis Chandler Museum**, 16, 17, 20, 21, 32, 33, 38, 39, 44, 45, 48, 49, 64, 65, 66, 67, 70, 71; **Leasha Overturf**, 162, 163; **Elizabeth Phillips**, 108, 109; **George Pilacek**, 152, 153; **Al Pinkus**, 232, 233; **Jim Rau**, 208, 209; **Claudio Rauzi**, 274, 275; **Paul Ross**, 54, 55, 146, 147; **Joe Rybacek**, 176, 177, 202, 203; **Steve Schifer**, 118, 119; **Robert Scott**, 138, 139; **Steve Searles**, 184, 185, 242, 243; **Cloyd H. Spahr**, 134, 135; **Bob Stark**, 76; **Al Steier**, 174, 175; **Robert Straka**, 296, 297; **Jody Synove**, 82, 83; **Anthony Tortoriello**, 302, 303; **Tom Turner**, 213; **Roger Van Etten**, 226, 227; **Buzz Walneck**, 150, 151, 180, 181; **The Estate of Garth Ware**, 206, 207; **Rick Weber**, 200, 201; **Larry and Caroline West**, 90, 91; **Jim Wetzel**, 160, 161; **Bill Yoakum**, 158, 159; **Rick Youngblood**, 188, 189

Contents

Contents *(continued)*

Foreword

Though most early motorcycles were essentially bicycles with small proprietary engines attached, the very first motorcycle, credited to Gottlieb Daimler and Paul Maybach of Germany, looked little like its successors. Built in 1885, it was a crude, wooden-framed contraption powered by a primitive gasoline engine and sup-

1885 Daimler (reproduction)

ported by a pair of training wheels, with the rider perched high on a thin leather saddle.

Like their automotive counterparts, numerous designs and powerplants were tried on early motorcycles. A few carried steam engines, though the weight and size of the necessary components quickly put this idea on the back burner. At least one mounted a radial engine *inside* the front wheel, which made for great traction and a simple driveline, but required the engine be stalled when coming to a stop. Even those that used conventional single-cylinder engines mounted them in different locations (sometimes over or beside the rear wheel), and fuel tank placement varied.

But by the early 1900s, most designs had reached a consensus: single-cylinder gasoline engine mounted between the frame downtubes with the fuel tank above it. Drive was typically by leather belt, with only one speed. Starting was accomplished by pedaling, either while on the center stand or going down the road.

Thanks to the availability of proprietary engines from De Dion of France, Minerva of Belgium, and others, most early motorcycles were produced by backyard mechanics. As such, anyone with a bicycle to start with could become a "manufacturer," and there were literally hundreds in the early part of the 20th Century.

However, competition weeded out most of these enterprises early on. As the surviving manufacturers tried to outdo one another, motorcycles became faster, more reliable, and more purpose-built, weaning themselves from their bicycle heritage. Engines gained more sophisticated intake and ignition systems, various forms of suspension were devised, drum brakes succeeded coaster brakes, transmissions and clutches were added, and kick levers replaced pedals for starting. Racing played a major role in these advancements, one of the oldest and most famous competitions being the Isle of Man Tourist Trophy race, held off the coast of England since 1907.

Then came World War I, which had a profound effect on motorcycling. The good news was that the war prompted engineering advances, but the bad news was that the wartime economy took its toll on several of the smaller makes. As a result, the state of technology advanced rapidly during the Teens, and machines built by the few survivors in the mid Twenties were surprisingly modern conveyances. Trouble was, a new and ominous foe was emerging.

Through the miracle of mass production, Henry Ford had been able to gradually decrease the cost of his Model T so that by 1925, prices were starting at less than $300—deep into motorcycle territory. Since it then became difficult to justify a motorcycle from a value standpoint, manufacturers began stressing the fun factor. Motorcycling became a "sport," and ads began touting the thrill and adventure of riding. This strategy seemed to work—right up until October 29, 1929.

The stock market crash had a devastating impact on all forms of business in the United States, and the motorcycle industry was no exception. Though the field had already narrowed considerably by that time, the Great Depression weeded out all the major American players save for Harley-Davidson and Indian.

Those two companies managed to hang on through World War II, during which both supplied motorcycles to Allied forces. After hostilities ceased, European motorcycles were exported to the U.S. in ever-growing numbers, and these posed yet another challenge to the two remaining American manufacturers—one of whom wouldn't survive.

Indian had been struggling since before the war, and was less able to face the onslaught of imports than was Harley-Davidson. It was a sad day when, in 1953, this venerable make finally closed its doors. U.S. importers tried slapping the name on a variety of smaller bikes over the years with little success, though a recent revival of a large American-built Indian V-twin seems to be gaining a foothold.

During the late Forties and early Fifties, motorcycling received a black eye from groups of enthusiasts who tended to get...well...a little too enthusiastic. So when Japanese manufacturers began exporting small motorcycles to the United States later in the Fifties, they were pushed as being more "friendly." "You meet the nicest people on a Honda" proved to be a strong advertising campaign, opening the floodgates for Japanese imports. Yet despite this influx of competitors during the postwar period, few great strides were made from an engineering standpoint. But that was all about to change—and it would change virtually overnight.

More than 30 years later, it's difficult to describe the impact the Honda CB750 had on the marketplace when it was introduced for 1969. Though it carried little in the way of new features, it made its mark by combining state-of-the-art technology with Japanese reliability, all at a reasonable price. Yet its place in motorcycle history is assured not so much for what it *was*, as for what it *did*.

The overwhelming success of the Honda 750 prompted other Japanese manufacturers to engage in a furious battle of one-upmanship. Ever larger and faster models appeared with typical Japanese reliability and low prices, and this sounded the death knell for the comparatively stagnant British motorcycle industry—and nearly did in Harley-Davidson as well.

But while the market was losing its British choices, it was gaining a wider variety of models. Scramblers, which were essentially street bikes mildly modified for off-pavement use, evolved into more specialized enduro and motocross machines. Cruisers offered custom styling right off the showroom floor. Long-distance riders found comfort in the new touring models, and high-performance sportbikes that mimicked fully faired racing machines became all the rage.

Virtually every industrialized nation has hosted a motorcycle manufacturer at one time or another, but only five countries produced machines that achieved international popularity: Germany, Great Britain, Italy, Japan, and the United States. All are represented here (along with a couple of other countries), and an effort has been made to include examples of the various styles of road-going motorcycles that eventually evolved, from low-slung cruisers to high-strung sportbikes.

So that the evolution of the motorcycle can be easily observed, entries are arranged chronologically, starting with the crude conveyances of the early 1900s and running through today's sophisticated machines. While the contents list reflects this progression, individual models can be found in the index under the manufacturer's name.

Today's machines are far quicker, safer, more comfortable, and more reliable than those of years past, yet their riders still enjoy the freedom and adventure felt by those hearty souls who made early motorcycles their transportation of choice. *Motorcycle Chronicle* celebrates some of the most memorable machines of the Twentieth Century, and salutes the riders—both past and present—who have made this sport what it is today.

1904 Indian

In the early 1900s, Oscar Hedstrom mounted a single-cylinder De Dion engine on a tandem bicycle for the purpose of pacing then-popular bicycle races. George Hendee, a bicycle manufacturer from Springfield, Massachusetts, saw the contraption at an event and proposed a cooperative effort to produce motorized bicycles commercially. Hedstrom agreed, and in 1901 the Indian Motorcycle Company was born.

Most pre-1910 motorcycles look as though the manufacturer simply bolted an engine and its accessories onto a common bicycle frame—which indeed was usually the case. But early Indians used the engine as a stressed frame member, effectively replacing the downtube beneath the seat. As with most motorcycles of the era, suspension was non-existent (save for the spring-mounted seat), and pedals were used to start the engine. However, Indian used a direct-drive chain rather than the more common tensioned leather belt to turn the rear wheel, the chain being more positive in operation—and more reliable.

This 1904 "humpback" is little different than the first 1901 models. Producing just over two horsepower, the 13-cubic-inch single provided a top speed of around 25 mph. Both the lubrication and ignition system were of the "total loss" variety. Braking was accomplished by backpedaling, which activated a rear coaster brake.

Dark blue was the color of choice until 1904, when black and vermillion became optional. The vermillion would later be known as "Indian Red."

1904 Marsh

The eastern coast of the U.S. was home to numerous motorcycle manufacturers in the industry's early days, and Marsh was one of the first. Located in Brockton, Massachusetts, the Marsh brothers built a motorized bicycle in 1899, with regular production commencing the following year.

Unlike many early manufacturers, which used engines built by outside suppliers, Marsh made its own. Like most powerplants of the day, it had a single cylinder with an intake valve opened by suction created when the piston was on its downward stroke (called an "atmospheric intake valve") and a mechanically actuated side exhaust valve. The spark plug was fired by a "total loss" ignition system, meaning there was no generator to recharge the battery; when it went dead, it was recharged by an outside source or replaced.

Though the first production engines produced less than two horsepower, a racing engine offering six horsepower was built in 1902. The motorcycle it powered could reach nearly 60 miles per hour, a blistering speed at the time.

In 1905, the Marsh brothers teamed up with Charles Metz and the resulting motorcycles were called Marsh & Metz, or just M.M. The company was among the first to offer a V-twin, that being a 45-degree unit that

arrived around 1906. Two years later, a 90-degree V-twin appeared, that was claimed to offer better internal balance.

But the pioneering manufacturer didn't last long. Like many others of the era, M.M. folded under the weight of stiff competition, closing its doors in 1913.

Typical for motorcycles of the period, neither the front nor rear offered any kind of suspension system, though the leather saddle was mounted on springs. Box beneath the seat carries the battery that powers the constant-loss ignition system; there is no generator. Chrome lever on side of fuel tank is the compression release, which cracks the exhaust valve open to ease starting. Like most engines of the day, the 27-cubic-inch (442-cc) single had an atmospheric overhead intake valve and mechanically activated side exhaust valve. Also common was the use of the engine as a structural frame member.

1910 Emblem

The Emblem Manufacturing Company was one of nearly 300 U.S. motorcycle producers in the early 1900s. Claiming "Class, Power, Speed & Satisfaction," Emblem had high hopes of achieving success in a crowded market.

The buyer of an Emblem in 1910 had several configurations from which to choose. The entry-level model was driven by a four-horsepower, single-cylinder engine that was fitted with V-belt drive and sold for $200. For $260, the top-of-the-line model came equipped with a seven-horsepower twin-cylinder engine that drove a flat belt with an adjustable idler wheel.

All Emblems were fitted with three batteries and a coil, but a Herz magneto could be added for an additional $25. For another $15, the owner could add the "Free Engine Pulley" option, which was an early attempt at a clutch mechanism. At the front, an enclosed coil spring controlled the motions of a leading-link fork, while a Troxel saddle mounted on compound springs handled the chores at the rear.

Emblems were sold in the U.S. between 1909 and 1918. But, like many other makes, the company fell victim to a depressed economy triggered by World War I. However, a 531-cc model was exported to Europe as late as 1925.

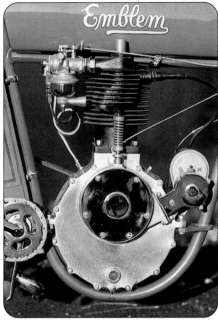

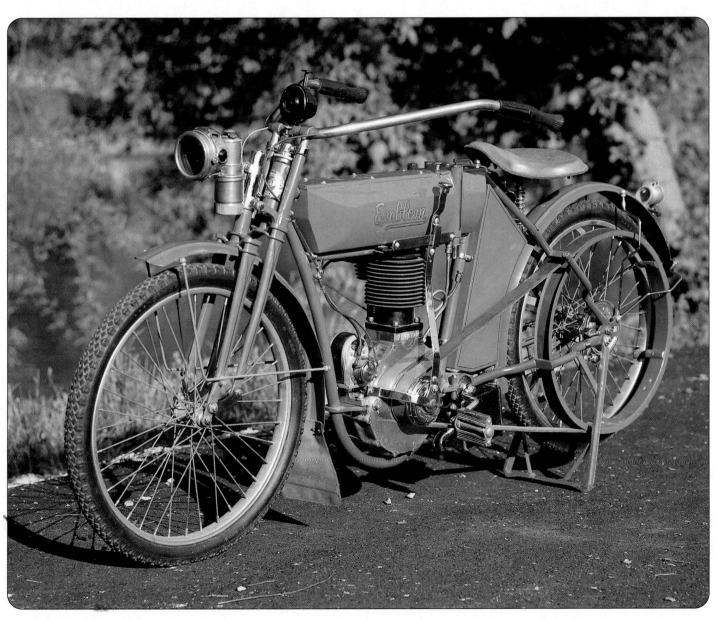

1910 Pierce

While most motorcycles of the era were powered by singles or the occasional V-twin, Pierce topped them all with America's first four-cylinder machine. Unfortunately, the design—and the company—would be short-lived.

Introduced in 1909, Pierce's four-cylinder model was influenced by the FN four built in Belgium. The low-slung Pierce, however, looked far more modern than the FN, and was a high-quality bike built around a heavy tubular frame that doubled as the fuel and oil tanks. Power came from a T-head engine displacing 700 ccs—about 42 cubic inches.

Pierce's four was a stately machine that was expensive to buy and even more expensive to build. The 700-cc flathead four was of T-head configuration, with the intake and exhaust valves on opposite sides of the cylinder. This resulted in a "crossflow" design that was theoretically more efficient than a conventional "side valve" engine with the two valves sitting next to each other. Fuel was carried in the top and rear frame tubes, oil in the front tube. Front suspension was a conventional leading link, but with an enclosed spring. Shaft drive was a first for American-made bikes.

It was a stressed part of the frame and drove the rear wheel through an enclosed shaft, another American first. Early models were direct drive, with no clutch and no gearbox; in 1910, a clutch and two-speed transmission were added.

Pierce's four was an expensive machine that saw limited sales. Though a less-expensive single-cylinder model of similar design was offered as well, both were rumored to cost more than their retail prices to build, and financial shortfalls forced the company to close its doors in 1913.

1911 Excelsior

Mr. Ignatz Schwinn had been in the business of building bicycles for several years when he decided to capitalize on the motorcycling craze that was sweeping the nation. By combining a 500-cc De Dion single-cylinder engine with a stout bicycle frame, Schwinn put the first Excelsior motorcycle on sale in 1908—or at least, the first Excelsior motorcycle to be built in the United States. Strangely, the name was already in use on motorcycles produced by separate companies in both Germany and England.

Although it produced some small two-strokes, Excelsior was better known for its four-stroke singles and V-twins, the latter arriving in 1910. All of the four-stroke models used F-head (overhead intake, side exhaust) engines of Excelsior's own design.

For 1911, the 30-cubic-inch single could be ordered with a choice of magneto or battery electrical system. The leading-link front fork provided only a small amount of travel, but that was more than was afforded by the rigid frame in back. As was common for the era, the single was driven by a wide leather belt, with progress slowed by a rear coaster brake.

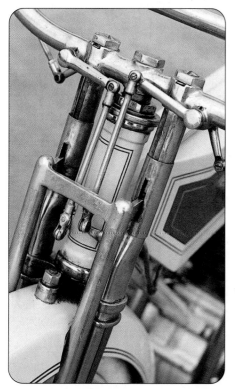

Before the advent of modern cables, control motions were transferred by intricate jointed shafts. Note fancy "engine-turned" finish on crankcase. The Excelsior's rear frame tube took a detour in order to clear the large drive pulley.

1911 Flying Merkel

In the early days of motorcycling, Merkels were the bikes to beat. Small singles of 1902 evolved into thundering V-twins by 1910, at which point the machines adopted the aptly descriptive "Flying Merkel" moniker.

The company was also known for innovation. Front forks that looked rigid were actually mounted on sliders with enclosed springs either at the top of the sliders or inside the frame neck. The design that became known as "Merkel-style forks" were popular add-ons to other manu-

Flying Merkels of 1911 offered V-twins of 885 and 1000 ccs, along with the customary single-speed belt drive. But these bikes were far ahead of their time in the suspension department, offering simple but effective "Merkel-style" forks in front, and a swingarm suspension in back.

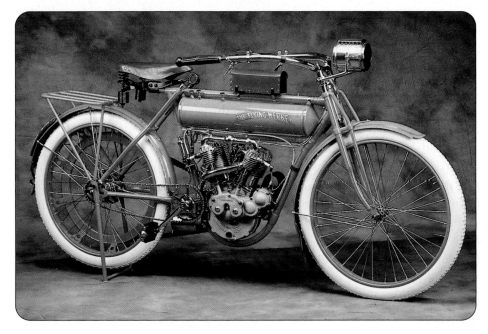

facturers' racing bikes. Merkel also was a pioneer in rear suspension; 1910 models offered modern swingarm designs incorporating sliders similar to those used on the forks.

None of this, however, was enough to keep the Flying Merkel aloft. Despite 1915 models that offered a kickstarter, front and rear suspension, sprung saddle, two-speed planetary transmission, and a powerful 1000-cc intake-over-exhaust V-twin, they would prove to be the final offerings of one of motorcycling's most innovative pioneers.

1912 Harley-Davidson X8A

Harley-Davidson's first motorcycle, little more than a bicycle with a single-cylinder three-horsepower engine mounted within the frame tubes, was built in 1903. Though the V-twins that would make the company famous appeared six years later, single-cylinder machines continued to represent the bulk of Harley's sales. By 1912, public demand for more power was answered with the X8A,

which was powered by a 30-cubic-inch single producing 4.3 horsepower.

A hand-operated oil pump was added to augment the existing gravity-feed system, and a magneto ignition was used for easier starting. Also new this year was the "Free Wheel Control," one of the industry's first clutch systems. With it, smooth takeoffs from a standing start were possible for the first time.

The issue of comfort was also addressed. Joining Harley's traditional leading-link front fork was the new "Full Floating" saddle, in which a coil spring mounted inside the vertical frame tube cushioned the seatpost, while the rear of the seat was supported by two more coils. Though this was hardly a substitute for a real rear suspension, it was as good as Harley riders would get for another 45 years.

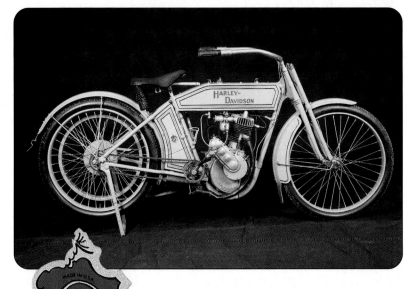

Tall lever on left side of tank activated the "Free Wheel Control," Harley's early clutch system. While many companies had gone to a mechanical intake valve by this time, the X8A stuck with an atmospheric intake valve, located beneath the small dome at the top of the engine's right side.

1913 Excelsior 7-C

Excelsior was once a big name in motorcycling, often ranking just behind Indian and Harley-Davidson in popularity. Since the company's inception in 1907 as a division of the larger Schwinn Bicycle concern, its motorcycles were in a constant state of improvement, as there was plenty of research and development talent on tap.

In 1910, the company's single-cylinder motorcycle was joined by an 800-cc V-twin. The V-twin soon grew to 1000 ccs and replaced the drive belt with a chain in 1913. By this time, the old leading-link forks had been supplanted by a trailing-link arrangement activating a leaf spring, but despite the added speed potential, the Excelsior still relied on a simple rear coaster brake. Soon afterward, a

three-speed transmission was adopted, replacing the former single-speed unit.

The next advancement was the "Big Valve Motor" using large 2⅛-inch valves, which brought the company a fair degree of racing success. With it, Excelsior officially broke the 100-mph barrier on a wooden track in 1912.

Since his interest in the world of motorcycles was growing,

Ignatz Schwinn purchased the financially troubled Henderson Company in 1917 and expanded his line to include Henderson's inline-four model. This new acquisition pushed the Excelsiors into the shadows as the big Henderson grew in popularity.

But just as quickly as the inspiration had come, Ignatz Schwinn seemed to lose interest in motorcycling. By 1931, both Henderson and Excelsior had joined the growing number of marques that had blossomed during motorcycling's boom years only to succumb to stiff competition and a depressed economy in the early '30s.

1913 Indian 61 Twin

Indian offered its first V-twin in 1907, a 40-cubic-inch (633-cc) unit with atmospheric intake valves, common at the time. By 1913, it had grown to 61 cubic inches and boasted overhead intake and side exhaust valves. Though standard models had but a single speed, a two-speed transmission was available as an option.

Indian built singles during this period as well, but the V-twin accounted for 90 percent of the company's production. It's not difficult to see why: In 1913, for example, a four-horsepower single cost $200, while a seven-horsepower twin went for $250—quite a performance bargain.

New for 1913 was a "Cradle Spring Frame" that incorporated the world's first swingarm rear suspension system—though it was somewhat different in design than what we commonly see today. When the rear wheel encountered a bump, two vertical rods actuated a pair of leaf springs attached to the frame beneath the seat. This joined a conventional (at least for Indian) trailing-link front fork that worked in a similar fashion. For those suspicious of the new technology, a rigid frame remained available. Braking was accomplished with an internal shoe/external band rear brake, which incidentally conformed to Britain's "dual brake" requirement for motorcycles sold in that country—though it might not have been exactly what the Brits had in mind.

Indian's swingarm rear suspension, which appeared in 1913, was an industry first. It joined a front suspension of similar design, both incorporating leaf springs. Further comforting the rider was a sprung saddle using—you guessed it—leaf springs. The upright cylindrical plunger beneath the seat is a small oil pump that allows the rider to feed more oil to the engine during periods of hard use or when traveling uphill.

1913 Reading Standard

Though Reading Standards first appeared in 1903 as little more than Indian knock-offs with a Thor motor, the company began building its own singles three years later, these being the first flatheads to be offered by an American manufacturer. V-twins arrived in 1908, and though early examples sported a more conventional F-head (overhead intake, side exhaust) configuration, the arrangement was unusual in that the valves were on the left side of the front cylinder, but on the right side of the rear cylinder. These first V-twins displaced 722 ccs, but had grown to 990 ccs when our featured 1913 model was built, by which time the company had converted its twins to a flat-head design. Later versions displaced as much as 1180 ccs.

Advertised as "R-S" motorcycles, Reading Standards were sold across the country. The company began entering competitive events in 1907, winning its first 1000-mile endurance race the same year.

By 1910, however, Reading Standard had tired of racing, and decided to focus its attention on selling more units at the retail level. Their decision was perhaps a bit late; by 1914, business had already begun to look grim.

In 1922, Reading Standard sold out to the Cleveland Motorcycle Company, which offered a Reading Standard model in 1923 as a low-dollar alternative to its existing line. The following year, however, Cleveland itself went up for sale, and the Reading Standard name slipped into oblivion.

An enclosed coil spring damped motion of the leading-link front fork. Like many bikes of the time, the "fuel tank" contained both gas and oil—in separate chambers. Along the side of the tank were (from front to back) the gas shut-off valve, gas cap, oil cap, regulator for oil drip to engine, and a pump to fill the oil reservoir. The Prest-O-Lite headlamp was fired by acetylene gas.

1914 Sears Deluxe

In the early catalogs from Sears and Roebuck, you could order almost anything—including a house. But it was in the 1912 catalog that Sears offered its first motorcycle.

This 1914 Magneto Model, complete with the 35-cubic-inch Deluxe "Big Five" engine, sold for $197.50 and was claimed to have nearly the same power as the larger twin-cylinder models. These single-cylinder versions were available with either batter-ies or a Bosch magneto. Two twin-cylinder motorcycles were offered, one producing seven horsepower, the other nine. The engines in all Sears machines were manufactured by Spake, which sold them to a variety of builders.

As with most makers of motor-cycles in this period, Sears claimed high quality and proven performance for its models. The handlebars were made of double-reinforced tubing and the fuel tank was formed out of anti-rust material. A trailing-link fork with leaf spring handled suspension chores in front, but a seat mount-ed on coil springs had to make do in the rear.

Sears only sold these early motorcycles until 1916, when they were removed from the cat-alog. But between 1953 and 1963, Sears offered a line of cycles manufactured by Puch under the Sears-Allstate mon-iker.

Tank-mounted speedometer is driven off a spiral gear on the rear hub. Sears used a trailing-link leaf-spring front suspension similar to Indian's.

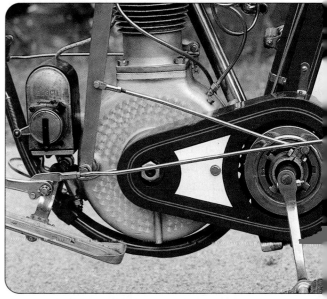

Bosch magneto sits ahead of the finely machined crankcase of the 35-cubic-inch Spake-built single. Lever beside the engine controls the clutch; pedal at lever's base activates the two-speed rear hub.

1914 Thor

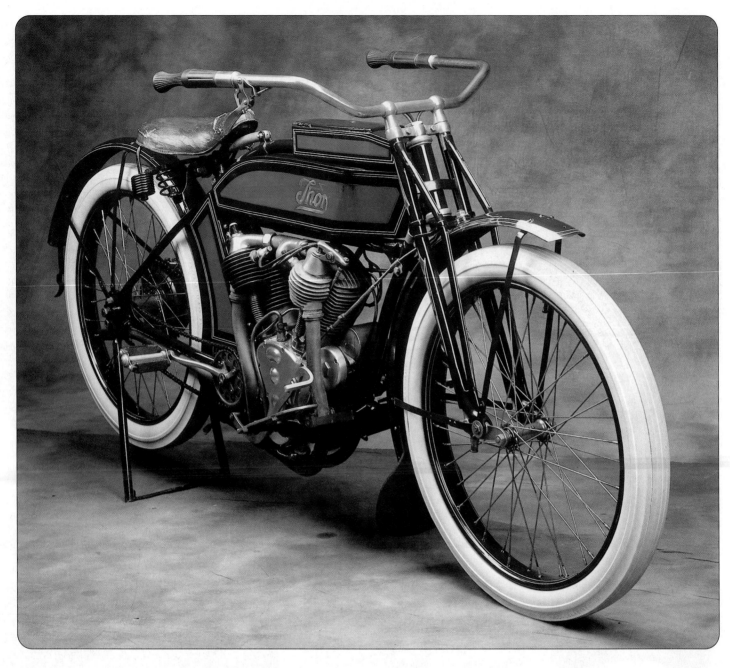

Thor played an instrumental role in the early years of motorcycle history, not for its machines as much as its engines. Many early manufacturers got their start mounting Thor powerplants in frames of their own choosing.

Owned by the Aurora Automatic Machinery Company, Thor began building engines for Indian in 1902. Later clients of note included Reading Standard and Sears, along with a host of lesser-known makes. When the contract with Indian ran out in 1907, Thor began building its own motorcycles. Early examples used a version of the Indian-designed single Thor had been producing for five years, and when Thor introduced its first V-twin in 1910, it was essentially the same engine with another cylinder bolted to the cases. But unlike most such designs, it was tilted forward so that the rear cylinder stood straight up, leaving room behind for the magneto and carburetor.

By 1913, Thor had introduced a new V-twin of its own design, and this one was mounted in the conventional manner. Displacing 76 cubic inches, it enjoyed some racing success, but was always in the shadows of Indian and Harley-Davidson on the track.

Like so many other manufacturers of the period, Thor eventually succumbed to a competitive environment. Its last motorcycles were built in 1917, after which the parent company concentrated on power tools and appliances.

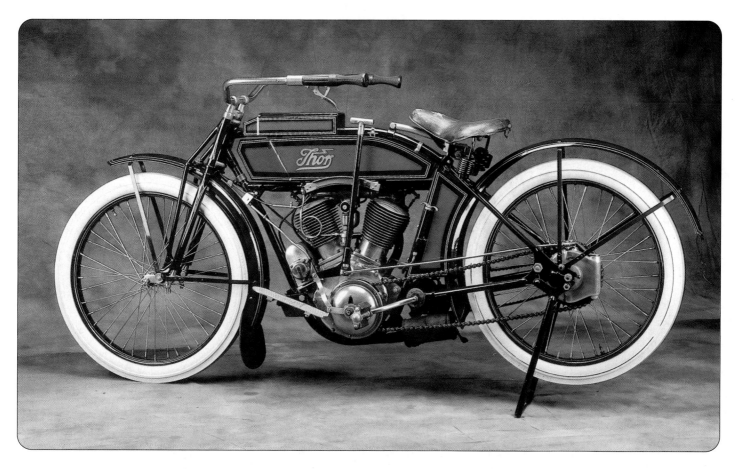

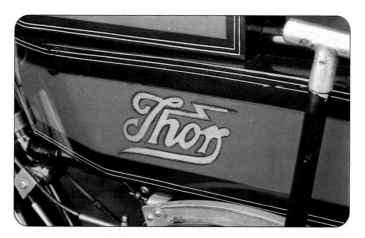

The V-twin was of convention intake-over-exhaust layout, but Thor ran the intake pushrods between the cylinder fins, where most manufacturers mounted them externally. Single and two-speed drive were offered, the latter shown here with its crankshaft-mounted transmission.

1915 Emblem Twin

By 1915, motorcycle manufacturers were springing up like weeds and a horsepower race was in progress. Each manufacturer claimed to outrun, outclimb, or outlast all the rest, and Emblem was no exception.

Emblem advertising that year stated that its twin displaced 76.6 cubic inches, "16 more than any other motorcycle motor." According to the Emblem sales brochures, each Emblem twin had to be ridden in excess of 70 miles per hour before it would be

shipped. A test card accompanying each bike indicated the speed that had been reached.

Emblem started out in 1907 with a single-cylinder machine, graduating to the big V-twin in 1913. Oddly, Emblem chose to reduce the displacement of its twins as time progressed, culminating in a lightweight 32-cubic-inch model for 1917. But that's not what American riders wanted, and most Emblems ended up being sold in export markets until the company's demise in 1925.

At 76.6 cubic inches, Emblem's V-twin was larger than others of the time, but was of conventional intake-over-exhaust design. Like many engines of the era, the overhead intake valves were actuated through exposed pushrods and rocker arms; the exhaust valve springs and pushrods can be seen flanking the exhaust pipes. Partially enclosed at the rear of the fuel tank is a hand pump used to feed additional oil to the engine under heavy load. Front suspension was the common leading link with coil spring, but the seat was cushioned with two large leaf springs and a sprung seatpost.

1915 Harley-Davidson 11F

Technology advanced rapidly at Harley-Davidson during the 1909-1915 time frame. The company's first V-twin arrived in 1909, though it was taken off the market in 1910 to fix some bugs and reintroduced the next year. This was followed by chain drive and one of the industry's first clutches in 1912, and a two-speed rear hub in 1914, which also saw the advent of floorboards and the Step Starter. For 1915, a proper three-speed transmission was offered, along with a magneto and electric lighting system incorporating a taillight that could be removed for use as a nighttime service light. The model shown, however, is equipped with a Prest-O-Lite headlight, which is powered by acetylene gas.

Harley-Davidson's 61-cubic-inch F-head V-twin,

while not a true overhead-valve design (only the intake was ohv), was more advanced than the flat-head engines that powered some competitors. Furthermore, the 1915 models gained an automatic oiler and larger intake valves, the latter helping to boost output to 11 horsepower. That rating, by the way, was guaranteed by Harley-Davidson, the only motorcycle manufacturer to back its quoted power claims in writing.

Elsewhere, the 11F was perhaps not so advanced. The expanding-band rear brake now featured double action to increase braking efficiency, yet was far from state-of-the-art, and the front suspension remained a leading-link arrangement with coil springs that allowed only slightly more wheel travel than the nonexistent rear suspension.

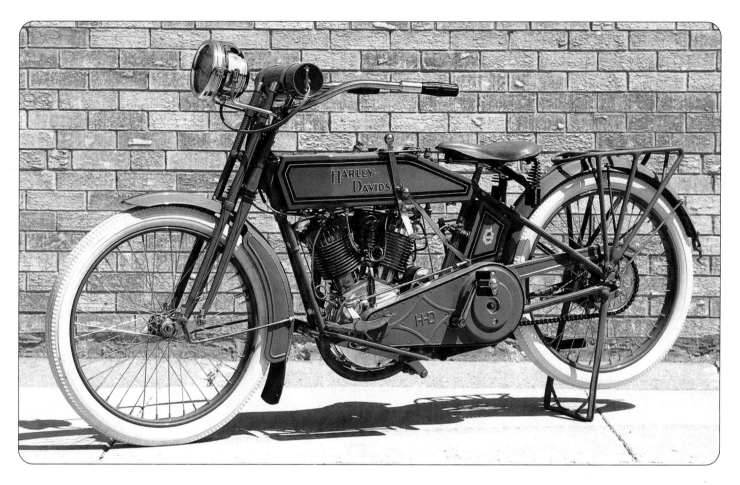

Electric lighting was newly available this year, but many riders had more faith in the old acetylene system. An exposed valvetrain was common in the era, and must have been fascinating—and messy—in action. View from the driver's seat, looking down at the fuel tank, which also carried oil. Shifter had a gated guide plate. Barely able to reach the handlebars, this little tyke is no doubt dreaming of the day he can ride a motorcycle of his own.

1915 Iver Johnson

Iver Johnson was best known for its bicycles and firearms when it branched out into motorcycle production in 1907. Though the line consisted of conventional singles and V-twins, many finer points of the machines differed from normal practice.

Most noticeable was Iver Johnson's use of dual curved upper frame tubes outlining the fuel tank that sat between them. Front suspensions were a leading link/leaf spring design similar in concept to Indian's, though the latter had a trailing link. Some models used the engine as a stressed frame member, and a few even offered a swingarm rear suspension.

Though Iver Johnson's V-twin was unusual in being a flathead design (Indians and Harley-Davidsons of the time were intake over exhaust), it was also a beautiful piece of work that unfortunately incorporated such features as an elaborately curved intake manifold that didn't help in the production of horsepower. As a result, despite displacing 1020 ccs, it wasn't particularly powerful compared with other V-twins, and that certainly didn't help Iver Johnson's status among power-hungry riders. At the end of the 1916 model year, the company abandoned motorcycles to concentrate on its firearms business, which continues to this day.

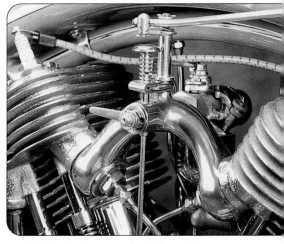

Though the gleaming intake manifold sure looked nice, the many changes of direction the intake charge had to make—most notably the sharp angle between manifold and head—was hardly beneficial to breathing. Painted crankcases were distinctive, as were the crankcase guards and cast floorboards.

1916 Harley-Davidson J

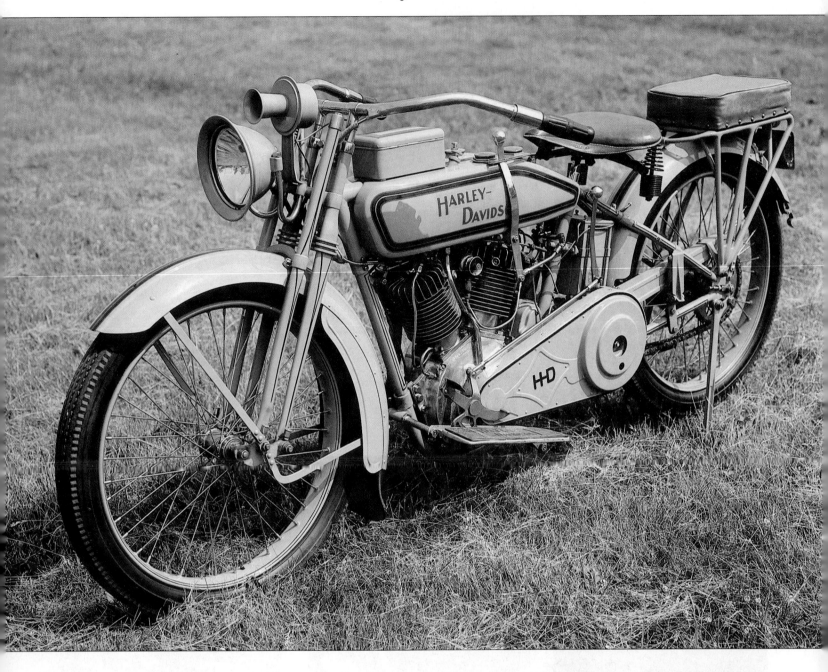

From a styling standpoint, the 1916 Harley-Davidsons were a great leap forward. Fuel tanks now had rounded rather than square-cut corners, and the whole bike took on a longer, lower appearance. Also, pedals no longer sprouted from the lower frame on models with the three-speed transmission, which now sported a modern kickstarter.

Other than the kickstarter, however, there were few mechanical changes of note. Forks remained a leading-link design with enclosed coil springs, and the 61-cubic-inch intake-over-exhaust V-twin received only a curved intake manifold to smooth the airflow into the cylinders.

This would be the last year Harleys would wear their traditional grey paint, which had graced the machines since 1906. Its replacement—Olive Drab—would be hardly more colorful, yet would enjoy an equally long tenure.

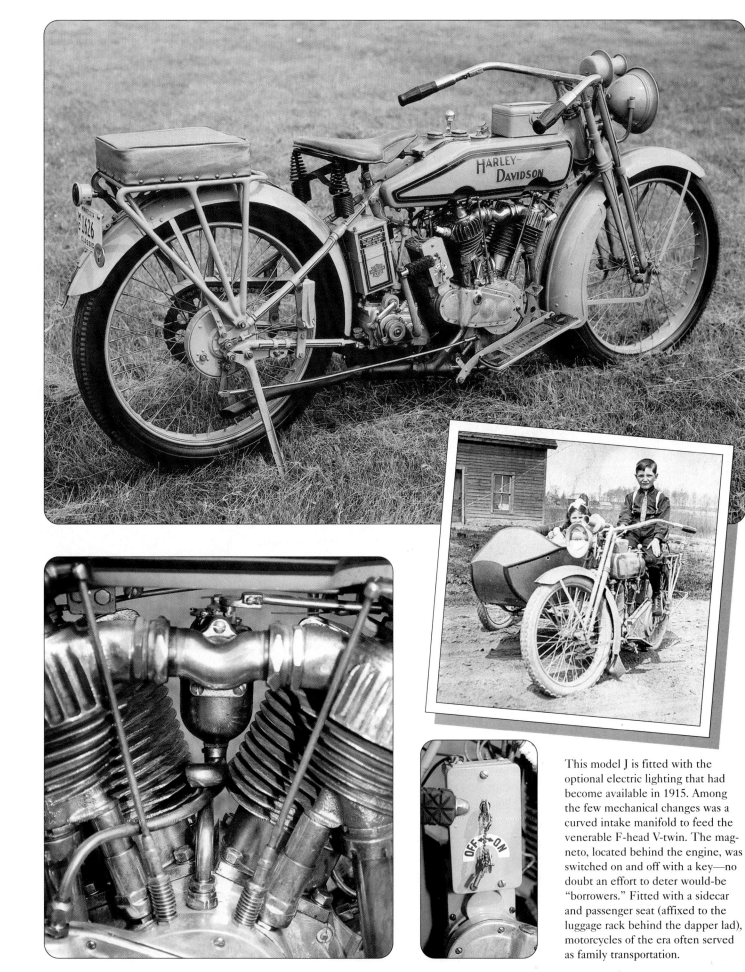

This model J is fitted with the optional electric lighting that had become available in 1915. Among the few mechanical changes was a curved intake manifold to feed the venerable F-head V-twin. The magneto, located behind the engine, was switched on and off with a key—no doubt an effort to deter would-be "borrowers." Fitted with a sidecar and passenger seat (affixed to the luggage rack behind the dapper lad), motorcycles of the era often served as family transportation.

1918 Pope L-18

Pope Manufacturing Company had been building Pope-Tribune automobiles and Columbia
bicycles for years before they combined the
two concepts and began producing motorcycles in
1911. Those early models were singles, but a V-twin
followed in 1912, and by 1918, Pope was known for
quality construction and innovative engineering.

This 61-cubic-inch V-twin illustrates the point
well. It features overhead valves at a time when
most competitors offered flathead or F-head engines. Crankcases were cast from an aluminum
alloy, and each set of pistons and connecting rods
were matched with another pair of the exact weight.
Its Armored Magneto ignition allowed use in all
types of weather.

The front suspension consisted of a trailing link

actuating a leaf spring. But perhaps the most
intriguing aspect of this Pope is the rear suspension.
Not only was having *any* rear suspension unusual at
that time, but the design was uniquely Pope. Unlike
the common swingarm that is used on motorcycles
today, Pope mounted the rear axle in a carrier that
moved up and down between two posts, compress-
ing a pair of springs on impact. Wheel travel was
minimal, but something was better than nothing,
and this became a major selling feature.

Unfortunately, this 1918 Pope represents the last
of the line. With World War I raging in Europe, Pope
suspended motorcycle production later that year to
concentrate on building machine guns, and after the
war, only the bicycle portion of the business was
revived.

1920 Ace

Brothers Tom and William Henderson began building their famous four-cylinder motorcycles in 1912, but after running into financial trouble, sold out in 1918 to Excelsior, the motorcycle arm of the Schwinn Bicycle Company. Yet within two years, William formed Ace to produce a similar four-cylinder motorcycle, though no parts were interchangeable with the Hendersons.

Ace produced a great product, but proved to be a short-lived proposition. The firm was suffering financial setbacks when William was killed in a motorcycle accident in 1922, and production ceased two years later. Indian Motorcycle Company purchased Ace in 1927, and continued to offer what was essentially the Ace four—wearing Indian logos, of course—until World War II.

The Ace was powered by an F-head inline four displacing 77 cubic inches. Power was transferred through a foot-operated multidisc wet clutch to a three-speed transmission with hand shift. The

leading-link front fork compressed a cartridge-type internal coil spring, but the rear wheel was attached to a rigid frame.

Weighing in at about 395 pounds, the Ace wasn't

particularly light, but proved to be both powerful and durable. Several transcontinental records were set on virtually stock machines, and a "hopped up" version called the XP4 set a record speed of 129 mph in 1923. The fact that this motorcycle continued in production for over two decades with little more than suspension and brake updates is further testament to its endearing design.

Like many bikes of the day, Ace used an external-contracting rear brake, where the friction band gripped the outside of a metal drum. There was no front brake. Ace's F-head inline four displaced 77 cubic inches, making it larger than most V-twins of the era. Cartridge-type internal coil spring gave a cleaner front-end appearance than did the exposed front springs of most competitors.

1925 Harley-Davidson JD

With the JD model of 1925, Harley-Davidson made great strides in modernizing its machines—at least from the standpoint of styling. A new frame placed the saddle three inches lower than before, wider but smaller-diameter tires gave the bike a huskier look, and the fuel tank took on a rounded teardrop shape. Color choices, however, remained the same as they had since 1917: anything the customer wanted,

as long as they wanted Olive Drab.

Since Harleys still lacked rear suspension, riders appreciated the softer fork springs and new contoured saddle, the latter of which also offered six-position height adjustment. The shift lever was moved farther forward along the side of the tank for convenience, and a fork-mounted tool kit made a debut appearance. Sidecars were popular accessories of the day, as these

vehicles often served as a family's primary form of motorized transportation.

The first of Harley's famed 74-cubic-inch V-twins was introduced in 1922 and continued with only minor changes through 1928. Some of those minor changes occurred in the JD: Iron alloy pistons replaced the previous aluminum slugs, and 16 Alemite fittings were added to the engine and gearbox to ease lubrication.

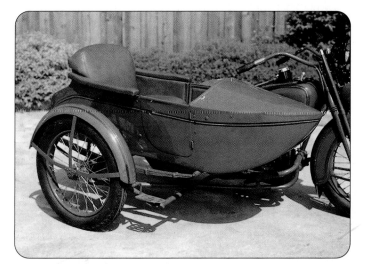

1926 Cleveland

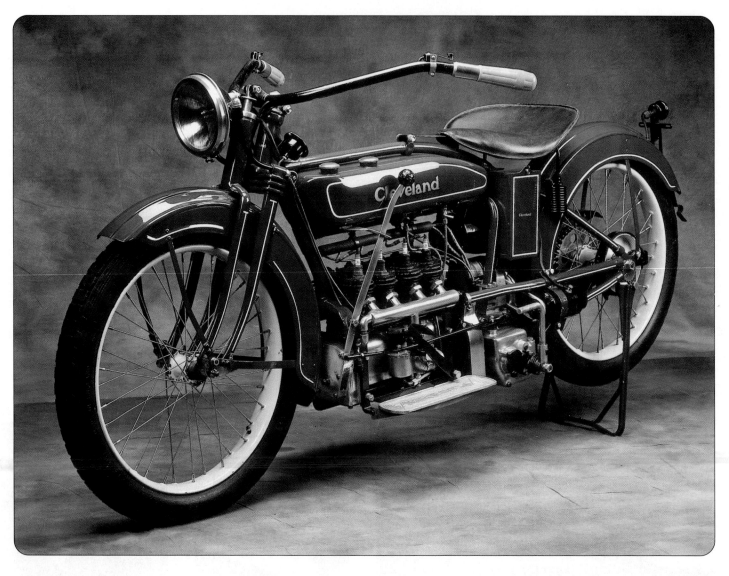

Cleveland bought into the motorcycle business in 1902 by slapping its name on a generic machine built by American Cycle Manufacturing Company. It was not alone. Columbia, Tribune, Rambler, and a host of others got started the same way—with essentially the same motorcycle. Aside from mounting the motor in a separate cradle between the diamond frame and rear wheel, these bikes were all very similar to Indians of the period.

Later Clevelands were more distinctive. Frames were long, low, and oddly configured, since they held a small two-stroke single that was mounted transverse-

ly with its crankshaft parallel to the bike's centerline. The two-speed transmission turned the power 90 degrees to culminate in chain drive to the rear wheel. Simple, light, and inexpensive, this model met with a fair degree of commercial success. But the market yearned for four-strokes, and Cleveland obliged.

After a brief run of four-stroke singles, Cleveland pulled out all the stops and introduced a four-cylinder model in 1926. Its 600-cc T-head engine (flathead with intake valve on one side of the cylinder, exhaust on the other) was much smaller than most fours, and even many V-twins. Like the singles that

preceded it, the crankshaft ran along the bike's centerline, but the transmission (now a three-speed) turned the power to allow for a chain-driven rear wheel—same as Ace, Henderson, and Indian fours, though some others used a shaft. Because of its small displacement, Cleveland's four was not an impressive performer, so it was quickly followed by a conventional flathead version that grew to 750 ccs and then 1000 ccs. Though the last, introduced in 1927, was the first production motorcycle with a front brake, its high price proved an insurmountable detriment when the Great Depression hit, and production ceased shortly thereafter.

At 600 ccs, Cleveland's four was smaller than most others, and performance wasn't up to the market's demands. Clutch pedal actuated an automotive-style clutch. Mounted just ahead of the fuel tank, oil-pressure and ammeter gauges were evidently considered more important than a speedometer—though the Cleveland wasn't that slow. Left-side shot reveals the shift lever, cast floorboard, updraft carburetor, rear-brake pedal, and behind the kickstarter, the generator, which was belt-driven off the magneto.

1926 Indian Prince

Indian's fortunes rose and fell during the Roaring Twenties, but in 1926 when this Prince was built, the company was on a high. Intended as an entry-level vehicle, the Prince was promoted on the slogan "You can learn to ride it in five minutes." Of course, Indian hoped those lured into motorcycling by the amiable Prince would return to buy a larger, more expensive Chief, or perhaps the soon-to-

be-released inline-four model.

With its 21-cubic-inch flat-head single and manageable 265-pound curb weight, the Prince made an ideal first motorcycle. Like most others of the period, it had a spring-mounted seat to make up for the lack of rear suspension. In front, girder-style forks compressed a coil spring to provide a nominal amount of suspension travel. Also common for the era was the

three-speed transmission and single drum brake fitted to the rear wheel.

A number of improvements marked the 1926 edition of the Prince. Most noticeable was the European-inspired rounded fuel tank that replaced the wedge-shaped tank used earlier. A redesigned saddle lowered the seat height a few inches, and handlebars were lengthened to reduce the long reach to the grips.

1927 Harley-Davidson BA

Though economical to buy and run, Harley's 21-cubic-inch single never sold particularly well during its ten-year production run. However, competition versions, known as "peashooters" due to the sound of their exhaust note, claimed many victories at the hands of Joe Petrali during the same period.

Two versions of the single were offered: a flathead with eight horsepower and an overhead-valve variant producing twelve horsepower—an impressive 50 percent increase. Yet the flathead sold better due to its lower cost and easier maintenance. Both could be fitted with electric lighting like the flathead shown.

America's preference for big, powerful twins led to the demise of these single-cylinder models in the mid Thirties. Harley continued for a time with a larger 30.5-cubic-inch single and made several later attempts at selling single-cylinder machines, but it was always V-twins for which the company was best known.

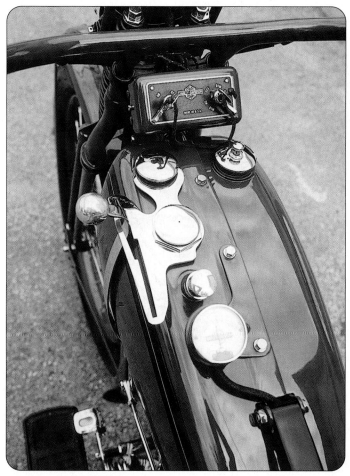

There was a lot of working room around the little 21-cubic-inch flathead single, which was a selling point in the late Twenties. Though front brakes were yet to appear at Harley-Davidson, the BA's external-band rear brake was sufficient for the bike's modest speed potential. "Big bike" features included leading-link front forks and three-speed transmission.

1934 Harley-Davidson VLD

Harley's traditional Olive Green paint—which had been used with little variation since 1917—was dropped as the standard color after 1932, to be replaced by more vibrant two-tones such as the black and Orlando Orange of our featured machine. Green, however, remained available for traditionalists.

Flathead V-twins, which had replaced F-head versions in the late Twenties, came in 45- and "Big Twin" 74-cubic-inch versions. These were landmark engines; the 45 would continue to power three-wheeled Servi-Cars into the Seventies, and the Big Twin would form the basis for the famous EL overhead-valve "Knucklehead" of 1936.

Triggered by a stock-market crash on October 29, 1929, the Great Depression killed off all the major U.S. motorcycle manufacturers save for Harley-Davidson and Indian—and despite decreased competition, even those makes teetered on the brink of extinction. But Harley had a strong dealer network and the right products at the right time, and things were beginning to look up by 1934.

Harley's two-place Buddy Seat with sprung seatpost arrived in 1933, quickly becoming one of the company's most popular accessories. Previously, passengers rode on a separate seat, usually mounted to the luggage rack.

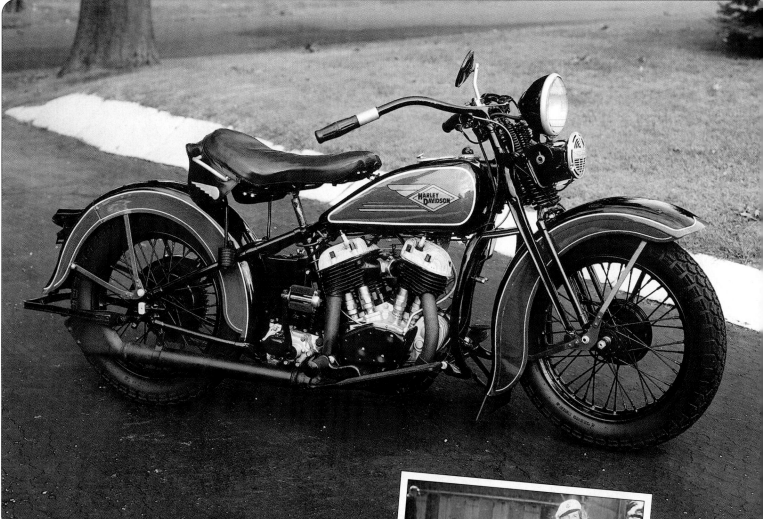

Despite the introduction of the more modern overhead-valve "Knucklehead" Big Twin in 1936, the flathead version would live on into the late forties. The sweep of the rear fender is accented by artful two-toning. Note hinge above the taillight; the rear part of the fender swings up to allow for tire changes. Horn is embossed with Harley's bar-and-shield logo. With her sailing cap at a jaunty tilt, this young lady looks ready to ride.

1935 Indian Chief

With the 1927 debut of the Ace-based four-cylinder model, the V-twin Chief was demoted to second fiddle in Indian's line. Yet the 74-cubic-inch Chief, which competed directly with the large Harley-Davidsons of the time, continued as the company's top seller.

The big Chief was anything but graceful in slow-paced maneuvers, its suspension design, long wheelbase, and 480-pound curb weight conspiring to make it feel clumsy around town. Once up to speed, however, these same features provided exceptional stability.

Buyers of a 1935 Chief were faced with a wide variety of options. Color choices were *reduced* that year to 13, though an extra $5.00 would buy any hue DuPont offered. Even the fuel and oil tanks were available in three different trim variations. An optional "Y" engine featured

aluminum cylinder heads, heavy-duty valve springs, and a modified muffler. A four-speed transmission could be ordered to replace the standard three-speed.

New to the '35 version were redesigned fenders with larger valances to smooth out the styling, and a rebound spring for the ungainly front leaf suspension that helped smooth out the ride somewhat. Chiefs still lacked any form of rear suspension, though they did offer a spring-loaded seatpost.

1936 DKW SB 500 A

German-based DKW began building motorcycles in 1919, starting with a one-horsepower engine in a bicycle frame. By the 1920s, the company had grown to become one of the largest producers of motorcycles in the world. Not only did DKW build its own machines, it also supplied two-stroke engines to other manufacturers, and even built automobiles from 1929 until the late Sixties.

Before the outbreak of World War II, DKW had amassed an impressive racing record, including a win at the Isle of Man TT event in 1938. During the war, DKWs saw extensive use on battlefields throughout Europe.

The 494-cc (30-cubic-inch) twin in the SB 500 A resulted from combining two separate 247-cc cylinders on a single block. Fed by a Bing carburetor, the two-stroke engine produced 15 horsepower. As did many bikes of the period, the DKW had a three-speed transmission with a hand shifter and foot-operated clutch. Also common for the era were the girder front fork and rigid rear frame.

"A" models differed from regular SB 500s in that they had a stronger frame fitted with a larger fuel tank and twin headlights. They also had electric start, a rare feature for that time; by contrast, Harley-Davidson didn't offer an electric starter until 1965.

1936 Harley-Davidson EL

Compared to the rampant speculation that preceded it, the official introduction of the 1936 EL was a bit anticlimactic. Dealers got the facts at their annual convention in December 1935, and though not as wild as the rumors had predicted, the 61-cubic-inch EL nevertheless set new standards for Harley-Davidson—not to mention the rest of the industry.

Most important was the V-twin's switch from a flathead design to overhead valves. Due to the resulting shape of the new rocker covers, the engine was dubbed "Knucklehead" by owners, a nickname by which it is still fondly known today. Equally significant was the new recirculating oiling system that eliminated the messiness and inconvenience of the previous "total loss" setup.

Unique to the 1936 EL are the rocker-shaft covers and air intake. The timing case cover was changed three times during the model year, each design a bit

The tank-mounted instrument panel, still a Harley styling element, included amp and oil-pressure readouts. "Knucklehead" nickname came from the engine's rocker-cover caps, which were originally round and held in with a screw, but were soon replaced by large hex-head bolts.

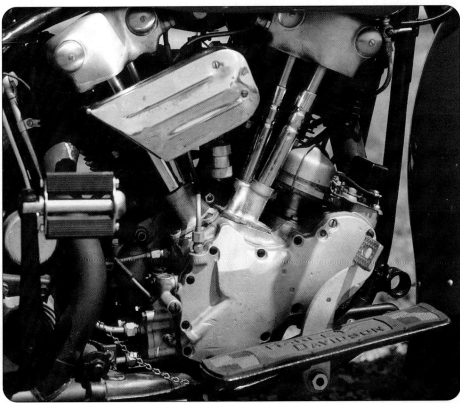

1936 Harley-Davidson EL

smoother than the last. Fuel tanks were welded and much sleeker than earlier examples, and the tank-mounted instrument cluster started a styling trend that continues to this day.

Despite the efficiency advantages of the EL's overhead-valve arrangement, Harley-Davidson continued to sell flathead V-twin motorcycles for many years to come. But the EL would go on to become one of the most popular Harley-Davidson models of all time, and its overhead-valve engine established a configuration that has been used for all the company's V-twins ever since.

This "Christmas" edition EL, above, displays one of the many color combinations available on Harleys of the era. Like most motorcycles of the day, Harleys used a hand shift/foot clutch arrangement; with shift lever all the way forward and "heel" down on the clutch pedal, the bike is shown in first gear with clutch disengaged. "Fishtail" muffler was another period styling touch, but was hard to see in basic black. Note frame-mounted tool box with Harley decal.

Harley-Davidsons have always been popular with police departments; this restored EL was originally put into service by the California Highway Patrol.

63

1937 Nimbus Luxus

The Danish-built Nimbus was offered only in four-cylinder/shaft-drive configuration throughout its 1920-1957 production span. While early models carried a flathead engine, overhead valves were in use by 1937.

Unusual Nimbus features exhibited here include a channel-steel frame (as opposed to round tubing), shaft drive, a fuel tank surrounded by the frame rails, and a centrally mounted gear lever situated behind the tank in its own console. The clutch could be operated by either a foot pedal or hand lever. Telescopic forks were unusual for the day, as were the pressed-steel handlebars. While both the driver and passenger seat were sprung, both were "hollow" underneath. The 45-cubic-inch overhead-valve four was of an efficient cross-flow design, but had exposed valve springs along with rocker arms that partially protruded from the head casting.

1938 Brough Superior SS 100

As the son of an early English motorcycle manufacturer, George Brough branched out on his own after World War I to build what would later be described as "the Rolls-Royce of motorcycles." These were expensive, well-finished machines compiled largely from proprietary components, most notably a 60-cubic-inch J.A.P. V-twin engine.

An early example was called the SS 80, so-named for its guaranteed top speed of 80 mph. Switching from flathead to overhead-valve engines brought the SS 100 in 1924. Though smaller V-twins and even a four-cylinder sidecar model with an Austin automotive drivetrain were offered, the company's legacy lies with its big V-twins.

The exemplary engineering and construction for which Brough Superiors were famous can be seen in our featured example's leading-link front suspension with driver-adjustable damping, nickel-plated side panels on the fuel tank, foot-operated gearshift, contoured saddlebags, and plunger rear suspension. Though renowned primarily for their fine craftsmanship, Brough Superiors also held many speed records during the Twenties and Thirties, culminating in a 1937 run of nearly 170 mph on—of course—a modified version.

In the annals of motorcycle history, Brough Superior will always be aligned with famed military figure and writer T. E. Lawrence—*Lawrence of Arabia*. Being a personal friend of George Brough, Lawrence owned several Brough Superiors, and sadly, died on one.

Smith's speedometer advanced in chronograph-like "clicks." Leading-link forks carried a separate rod tied to a driver-adjustable leather-faced damper. Even the gas caps and "fishtail" muffler pipes exuded quality.

1938 Harley-Davidson UL

After recovering from a difficult period in the early Thirties, Harley-Davidson was poised to forge ahead with a complete lineup that included 11 different models. It was built around "Big Twin" engines of 61, 74, or 80 cubic inches, all of which shared several components. However, the 61-cubic-inch V-twin was the famous "Knuckle-head" with overhead valves, while the 74- and 80-cubic-inch V-twins had side valves.

The UL was a Sport Solo model with a 74-cubic-inch flathead powerplant. Flatheads had been modernized in 1937 with the adoption of the recirculating oiling system introduced on the Knucklehead the year before, and in 1938 gained more subtle changes: Higher handlebars resulted in a more comfortable riding position, the instrument panel was simplified by replacing the ammeter with a red warning lamp and the oil-pressure gauge with a green lamp, and new colors and striping were made available.

Surprisingly, Big Twin flatheads remained in the Harley line for a dozen years after the debut of the famed Knucklehead overhead-valve models. And the smaller 45-cubic-inch flathead V-twin continued to power three-wheeled Servi-Cars into the Seventies—both indications that many riders continued to admire the inherent simplicity of the flathead design.

1940 Crocker

In a discussion of post-Depression American V-twins, Harley-Davidson and Indian are undoubtedly the best-known makes. But in terms of performance, neither could hold a candle to a Crocker.

While the original Crockers were single-cylinder speedway machines, the first production models were large-displacement V-twins. Manufactured in Los Angeles, California, from 1936 to 1940, only 61 Crocker V-twins were built, making the survivors very rare indeed.

Contrary to some rumors, the Crocker used no Indian or Harley-Davidson components. Albert Crocker had enough experience to design and produce most of the parts at the company's Los Angeles location. Since Crockers were built to special order, displacement was up to the customer; some engines were as large as 100 cubic inches.

However, all Crocker production V-twins had overhead valves; early models had a hemispherical head with exposed valve springs, while later models had a flat, squish-type combustion chamber with enclosed valve springs. Most were magneto-fired, with carburetors by Linkert or Schebler. All came with a nearly indestructible three-speed transmission, the housing for which was cast into the frame.

Two different V-twins were offered: a Big Tank model and a Small Tank version, both fuel tanks being made of cast aluminum. The latter could be easily identified by the two mounting bolts that ran all the way through the tank halves. It also had a more upright fork angle that shortened the wheelbase and quickened the steering, making it better suited to racing.

On the street, at least, Crockers were formidable machines, able to humble most other bikes of the era. But due to their small numbers, few riders ever saw one—which is just as well, considering the humiliation that could follow.

1940 Indian 440

Indian began offering inline fours after acquiring the Ace Company in 1927, and the first examples were little more than Aces with red paint and Indian logos on their tanks. The engine had overhead intake valves and side (flathead) exhaust valves, a configuration known as an F-head.

This four-cylinder model remained virtually unchanged until 1936, when the valve layout was reversed in an effort to wring more power from the 77 cubic inches. Often referred to as the "upside-down Indian," the new model was a dismal failure.

Maintenance was more difficult than before and overheating became a problem, so Indian reverted to the original design two years later.

The 1940 version, called the 440, adopted skirted fenders that added a more streamlined look. They also added about 36 pounds to the already imposing mass that totaled 568 pounds. But the 440 boasted not only the typical Indian leaf-spring front suspension but also an atypical coil-spring rear suspension, and, if anything, the added weight made it ride more smoothly than ever.

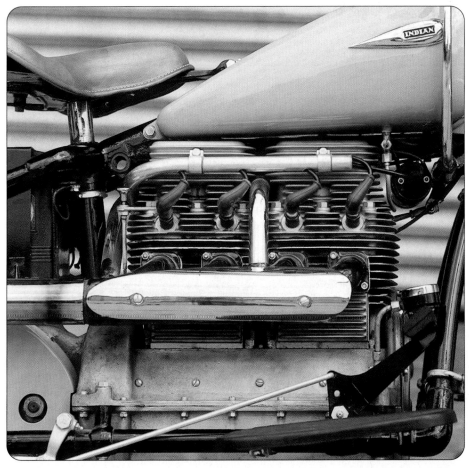

With a list price in 1940 of over $1000 (a new Chevrolet could be purchased that year for less than $700), Indian Fours were not high-volume sellers. In fact, a total of only about 10,000 were built during the model's entire 15-year production run.

1942 Harley-Davidson WLA and XA

Model WLA

Though rival Indian also supplied motorcycles to the U.S. military during World War II, the majority of those used in battle were Harley-Davidson WLAs. Wearing the requisite Olive Drab paint, these were 45-cubic-inch V-twins fitted with special equipment for wartime use. Items such as an ammo box, machine-gun scabbard, and rear carrier are obvious; less so are the special "blackout lights" front and rear that projected only a small sliver of light in an effort to avoid detection. In all, roughly 80,000 WLAs were built, many being sold as surplus after the war. These were often stripped down and fitted with aftermarket parts, fueling the rapidly developing customizing trend.

The small blackout light on the front fender was used when concealment was necessary; a similar taillight is found at the rear. A metal plate engraved with pertinent maintenance data was mounted on top of the fuel tank for quick reference.

Model XA

Harley's XA, with its horizontally opposed twin and shaft drive, was designed for desert warfare, but never was used in combat. Note the shock absorber added to the front suspension.

Rare when new—and even more so today—was the Harley XA that was intended for desert use. In a vast departure for Harley-Davidson, the engine was a horizontally opposed twin—similar to BMWs of the day—and it drove the rear wheel through a foot shift transmission with hand clutch (production

Harleys of the day were all hand shift/foot clutch) and a jointed shaft instead of a chain. A girder-style fork handled suspension chores in front, while at the rear was a "plunger" suspension as used on contemporary Indians. However, only 1000 XAs were built, and none saw service overseas.

1946 Indian Chief

When Indian resumed production after the war, the four-cylinder and smaller V-twin models were relegated to history, leaving only the now-legendary V-twin Chief. These machines were similar to prewar versions; the engine remained a 74-cubic-inch flathead and tank graphics were unchanged. As always, "Indian Red" was a popular color choice, though others—including two-tones—were available.

New, however, were girder-style coil-spring front forks adopted from

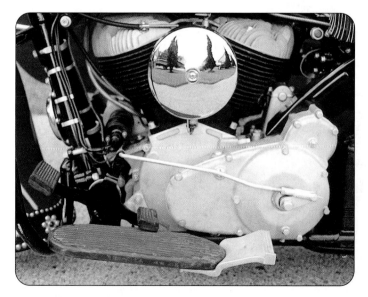

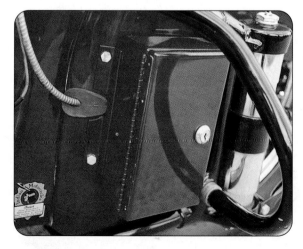

Front and rear crash bars and a locking tool box were
popular accessories of the day.

1946 Indian Chief

Indian's radical 841 model that had been designed for desert use by the U.S. military during the war. These new forks provided a full five inches of wheel travel versus the meager two inches allowed by the previous leaf-spring design. Though the rear still featured the same plunger-type suspension, spring rates were softened. These changes resulted in an even smoother ride than before, a notable selling feature of the postwar models.

Another accessory was a spring-mounted sidecar, first offered in 1940, which carried fancy chrome speedlines and trim. Two-tone color schemes could be substituted for the traditional Indian Red.

1947 Triumph Speed Twin

Like so many other early makes, the Triumph nameplate was originally affixed to a line of bicycles that came out in the late 1800s. In 1902, the company began bolting small, Belgian-made Minerva engines into the frames, and the Triumph legacy was born.

Based in Coventry, England, Triumph offered nothing but single-cylinder motorcycles in its early years. Though a two-cylinder model had gotten as far as the experimentation stage in the early Teens, the first of Triumph's famous vertical twins didn't go on sale until much later.

In 1936, Edward Turner joined Triumph as its chief designer and general manager. He quickly went to work developing a new, lightweight two-cylinder motorcycle, and within two years the company introduced a landmark machine: the Speed Twin.

First shown in late 1937 and sold as a 1938 model, the Speed Twin featured a 500-cc engine and four-speed transmission that were carried in separate cases—a simple design that would be used in several

Triumph models over the years. Blessed with decent power and a light chassis, the Speed Twin was not only the mount of choice for numerous police departments throughout Europe, but was the template used to spawn a generation of English bikes.

Modern telescopic forks handled suspension chores in front fairly well, but the sprung saddle was the only rear suspension offered, as the Speed Twin rode a rigid frame. In 1947 an optional sprung rear hub was offered, and our featured Speed Twin is so equipped. But it turned out to be a disappointment to those who ordered it, for the design allowed only minimal travel while adding a complex inner assembly of springs and related hardware.

Speed Twin carried a speedometer, ammeter, and light switch in the headlight bezel. In the mid Sixties, Triumph joined other manufacturers by combining engines and transmissions into one unit, which resulted in a more compact design. Today, however, "pre-unit" Triumphs are highly coveted in the collector market. Triumph's sprung rear hub, first offered as an option in 1947, afforded only about one inch of wheel travel—hardly a substitute for a good swingarm suspension.

1948 Harley-Davidson FL

At Harley-Davidson, changes came thick and fast in the postwar years. Though 1948 saw the opening of a huge new engine production facility in Wauwatosa, Wisconsin, a few miles west of the Milwaukee facility, that year's biggest news—at least to collectors—came in the form of Harley's new FL model with its "Panhead" V-twin.

Replacing both the 61-cubic-inch overhead-valve Knucklehead and the 74-cubic-inch flathead V-twins, the overhead-valve Panhead was available in the same two displacements and incorporated several improvements. Beneath its roasting-pan-shaped rocker covers (from which it got its nickname) lay aluminum heads that were lighter and provided better cooling than their cast-iron predecessors. Hydraulic lifters reduced valve noise and eliminated most adjustments, while an improved oil circulation system resulted in longer engine life.

There were other changes as well. More chrome trim pieces gave the bikes a fancier look, and a steering-head lock was added in case the extra flash attracted the wrong kind of attention. A latex-filled saddle was optional, as were eight equipment packages that let buyers tailor an FL to their own tastes.

Apparently, these changes were appreciated by the motorcycling public, for Harley-Davidson sold a record 31,163 units in 1948. But more big news was on the horizon....

Harley introduced the "Panhead" Big Twin for 1948 in a motorcycle that was otherwise little changed. Serrated exhaust pipes would continue into the Seventies. As before, the front fender light served fashion more than function, but was a notable styling feature. "Tombstone" taillight introduced in the Forties lasted through '54, and remains popular with customizers.

1948 Harley-Davidson S-125

At the close of World War II, thousands of G.I.s returned to the states hungry for transportation. Many had seen or spent time on Harley-Davidson's WLA military motorcycles in use overseas and now craved one of their own. With finances being tight for many, Harley decided to build a small, inexpensive machine for the masses. The result was the S-125.

With a single-cylinder two-stroke engine designed by DKW of Germany, this was not the kind of motorcycle most people associated with Harley-Davidson. Yet the company claims that 10,000 were sold in the first seven months of 1947.

Producing only three horsepower, the S-125 had a tough time reaching 55 miles per hour. Though a girder fork with coil spring was used up front, the rear had no suspension—other than what was provided by the sprung saddle. But with a three-speed gearbox, foot shift, and hand clutch, the lightweight bike was simple and easy to operate. Many were "personalized" by adding the optional chrome wheel rims.

Several changes benefited the little Harley during its 13-year life span. Most notable was a switch to modern "Teleglide" telescopic forks in 1951, and a boost in engine size to 165 ccs in 1954. The following year the bike became known as the Hummer, and it continued with only minor updates through 1959, after which it was dropped in favor of more contemporary designs.

Girder-style front fork was part of the original DKW design and wasn't used on other Harleys. Modern hand clutch/foot shift was common in Europe at this time, but a first for Harley-Davidson street bikes; only the wartime XA—of which but a thousand were built—preceded it. Harley's traditional horn was fitted to the S-125, though in a rather odd place.

1948 Harley-Davidson WL

Harley-Davidson's first flathead V-twin appeared in 1929 as the Model D. Its 45-cubic-inch engine was smaller than the company's existing 61- and 74-cubic-inch F-head V-twins, which then became known as "Big Twins." The latter switched to a flathead design the following year, but those larger engines were neither as reliable nor as long-lived as the understressed "Forty-five."

Though the Forty-five was no powerhouse, it proved to be a versatile engine that remained in production for more than four decades. During that time it served duty not only in street motorcycles, but also in three-wheeled Servi-Cars (1933-1973), military WLAs of the Forties, and WR racing bikes of the Forties and Fifties.

By 1948, the Forty-five was powering a street model called the WL. It looked very similar to Harley's Big Twin flatheads of the era, the most noticeable visual difference being that WLs had their drive chains on the right side of the bike, while

Big Twins had them on the left. Though 1948 would prove to be the final year for Big Twin flatheads, the WL lasted through 1951, after which it was replaced by the K-series carrying a redesigned 45-cubic-inch flathead V-twin with unit construction (motor and transmission in one case).

Like its larger stablemates, the 45-cubic-inch WL carried a tank-mounted instrument panel. It continued with Harley's hand-shift/foot-clutch arrangement, but by this time, the pattern was reversed so that first gear was closest to the rider. What the Forty-five lacked in power it made up for in persistence. Known for its durability, the engine was produced from 1929 through 1973, spending the second half of its life powering the three-wheeled Servi-Car exclusively. Yet this pedestrian flathead V-twin also powered one of Harley's more successful racing bikes, the WR. Intended for dirt tracks, the WR's trump card was a broad powerband that minimized the necessity to shift gears. Introduced after the war and competitive into the Fifties, it came from the factory in racing trim, meaning no lights, no horn, no fenders...and no brakes.

Servi-Car

Model WR

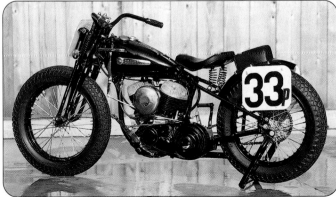

1949 BSA B33

As one of England's oldest motorcycle companies, BSA grew out of a consortium of firearms manufacturers who first expanded into bicycles, then into the fledgling "motor bicycle" market by fitting a stronger frame with a Belgian-made Minerva engine. That was in 1905; by 1910, Birmingham Small Arms was building its own 30-cubic-inch flathead single, and BSA was on its way to becoming a household name.

Though the company also built large V-twins for 20 years before World War II, its stock in trade remained midsize singles. These were often available at bargain prices and thus sold in large volume. During the war, BSA supplied over 120,000 of its M20 500-cc flathead singles to Allied forces, where their simple mechanics made them reliable and easy to repair. While contests of speed were typically won by other makes, BSAs had more than their share of success in endurance races, furthering their reputation for toughness that carried far more appeal to the everyday rider.

Typical of early postwar BSAs is the B33, which arrived in 1947 with a 500-cc (30-cubic-inch) overhead-valve single. Simple and stout, it formed the basis for a series of similar machines that carried on through the Fifties. Modern telescopic forks were used in front, but early versions had a rigid frame and thus no rear suspension save for the sprung saddle.

Vertical twins joined the line after the war and became legends in their own right. And adding those to an early-Fifties selection of popular small- to large-displacement singles briefly made BSA the largest motorcycle company in the world.

Instrumentation was simple and sparse. Tall "chimney" on the side of the engine enclosed pushrods for the B33's overhead valves. Notch in the rear of the fuel tank accommodates the seat.

1949 Harley-Davidson FL Hydra-Glide

After bringing out the refined Panhead engine the previous year, Harley's big news for 1949 was the introduction of "Hydra-Glide" front forks. Replacing the former leading-link forks, Hydra-Glide was a modern telescopic design that provided greater travel and a much higher level of riding comfort. However, the frame still lacked any form of rear suspension; that would take another few years to develop.

The big Harleys were now called "Hydra-Glide" in reference to the new forks, marking the first time

they carried a name as well as a series designation. They remained available in 61-cubic-inch EL and 74-cubic-inch FL versions, and though the latter is represented here, there was little difference in appearance.

The 1949 FL was not only more comfortable to ride, but also easier to stop due to a larger front brake. Though by this time many motorcycles were adopting foot-shift transmissions, that too was some time off for the big FL series, which still made use of a hand shifter and foot clutch.

Tank-mounted instrument panel remained a styling element. Note overload spring that could be swung into place to assist the sprung seatpost when a passenger or heavier rider was aboard. Attached to the new front end were handlebars that could be adjusted for position—a novel concept in the Forties. Note the now-classic bucket headlight and backing plate that appeared on the Hydra-Glide. Chrome trim, which in this case included speedlines, fendertips, and toolbox cover, was a popular accessory.

1951 Vincent HRD Series B Rapide

After purchasing the HRD company in 1928, Philip Vincent added the name to his own line of motorcycles. As an inventor and engineer, Mr. Vincent produced some very innovative designs during his career, and bikes carrying the Vincent HRD logo were known for their quality construction—and high prices. It was the latter that would lead to the company's demise in 1955.

Vincent's first models were powered by engines produced by the J.A.P. company (as were many other motorcycles of the era), and sported rear suspensions—unusual for the day. But in 1935 the company introduced its own engine, a 500-cc overhead-valve single. V-twins followed, essentially being two singles combined on a common crankcase.

The early V-twin, mounted in a motorcycle called the Series A 1000, gained the nickname "plumber's nightmare" due to its spaghetti-like web of external oil lines. After World War II, the Series B Rapide appeared with a cleaner design. The new motor was a 50-degree V-twin that doubled as a structural frame member; gone were the front and rear downtubes of older models.

Postwar Vincents, therefore, looked a bit odd, as though all the individual components were bolted to each other rather than to a skeletal frame—which, in essence, they were. "Girdraulic" front forks were unusual in that they combined a girder design with a shock absorber. Rear suspension was also unique, as a triangulated swingarm compressed dual coil-over shocks mounted beneath the seat. But most important to buyers was that Vincents were the fastest bikes of their day, though admittedly their 1000-cc engines were larger than those of most European competitors.

In 1949, a high-performance

Depicted on this postcard is Rollie Free running a Vincent Black Shadow at Bonneville. As the story goes, after reaching 148 mph in the "normal" riding position, Free stripped down to swim trunks and swim cap and laid horizontally across the rear fender in an effort to reach 150—which he did. For this postcard, however, he was dressed in painted-on clothes and helmet.

version of the Rapide joined the line. Called the Series C Black Shadow, it had black-painted engine cases and was even faster than the Rapide, and today is one of the most coveted classic motorcycles in the world.

Triangulated swingarm compressed twin shocks mounted below the saddle. Note the quick-release rear wheel, which had different size sprockets on each side and could be reversed to change gear ratios.

1951 Whizzer Pacemaker

Though perhaps more "motorbike" than "motorcycle," Whizzer's contribution to the sport centers more on what it did than what is was.

In the late 1930s, Whizzer began providing a kit whereby anyone with $80 and a bicycle could experience the thrill of motorized travel. Not fast travel, mind you, but faster than their legs alone could take them. Typically affixed to Schwinn bicycles, these kits included a two-horsepower flathead engine and associated drive accessories that allowed speeds over 30 mph.

After the war, Whizzer produced a vastly more powerful engine—now a raging *three*

horsepower—and eventually offered them in complete machines. These were Whizzer Pacemakers, which could be fitted with all manner of ritzy accessories, including "dual" exhausts. Many an enthusiast cut their riding teeth on Whizzers in the early Fifties, the experience often encouraging them to progress to larger mounts.

Whether the company's popularity helped incite the scooter trend in the late '50s is hard to say, but if so, Whizzer became a victim of its own success. With the flood of imported scooters and mopeds that swept the country in the '60s, Whizzer faced competition it couldn't underprice, and the company closed its doors in 1962.

Whizzer's initial 138-cc (8.5-cubic-inch) flathead single supplied two horsepower; a later 199-cc version upped that to three. Pacemakers featured a rudimentary telescopic front fork. Accessories were plentiful; among those shown are chrome headlight and taillight, chrome fuel tank, speedometer, chrome luggage rack, light-up rods on rear fender, and chrome fender tips. Kits to convert any "man's balloon-tire bike" continued to be offered even after the Pacemaker was introduced.

1952 Triumph Thunderbird

Any foreign manufacturer that exports to the U.S. has to listen carefully to the changing demands of the marketplace, and that's just what Triumph did when it released the 6T in 1950.

While the company's offerings were generally well received in postwar America, there was a cry for more power from those accustomed to large-displacement Indians and Harley-Davidsons. And though the 6T's 650-cc engine was barely half the size of the thunderous V-twins of those rivals, it was at least a step in the right direction.

Triumph's popular Speed Twin was the basis for the 6T, and their engines looked the same from the outside. But it was what was inside that made the difference: Some minor modifications and an extra

150 ccs of displacement netted eight more horse-power, raising the total to 34.

New, too, was the styling. A monotone paint scheme bathed frame, tanks, forks, fenders, and even wheel rims in the same color, while new badges and a luggage rack graced the fuel tank. The headlamp was housed in a streamlined nacelle that tapered into the telescopic front forks, and speed-lines were added to fenders, the nacelle, and as part of the badge on the fuel tank.

As was Triumph's custom, the 6T was given a "stage name" in addition to its alphanumeric designation, and Thunderbird became the chosen moniker—this, of course, years before it was applied to Ford's two-seat sports car.

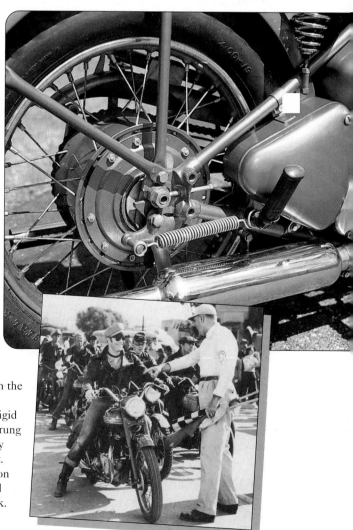

A Triumph Thunderbird was Marlon Brando's mount in the 1954 film, *The Wild One*. While modern telescopic forks were found in front, some Triumphs of the era used a rigid rear frame with a sprung hub in the rear wheel. The sprung hub was a complex mechanical device that allowed only about one inch of wheel travel—hardly worth the effort. Pre-unit Triumphs, in which the engine and transmission were housed in separate cases, had an oil tank mounted beneath the seat. The transmission is below the oil tank.

1953 Indian Chief

Though Indian had enjoyed a long and rich history, financial problems beset the company in the early Fifties. Attempts at postwar singles and vertical twins intended to compete with the machines from Europe ultimately proved unsuccessful, and their development had cost the company dearly.

By 1953, the sole surviving Indian was the V-twin Chief, and despite Indian's monetary crisis, it had seen a fair number of updates during the postwar years. Modern telescopic forks replaced the girder front end in 1950, when the 74-cubic-inch V-twin was enlarged to 80 cubic inches. In 1952, the front fender was trimmed to a thinner contour and a cowling was added on top of the forks.

The Chief's flathead V-twin was considered somewhat archaic compared to Harley-Davidson's overhead-valve engines, but the Indian used a more modern ignition system. Whereas Harleys had a single coil that fired both plugs at the same time once per revolution (one plug firing needlessly), Indian used an automotive-type distributor that fired each plug only on its cylinder's power stroke. This was hardly an overwhelming advantage, however.

According to factory records, 700 Chiefs were built in 1952, while only 600 were completed in 1953. After that, the Chief—and Indian along with it—was relegated to history, leaving Harley-Davidson the sole surviving American motorcycle manufacturer.

With its massive skirted fenders, locomotive-like torque, and "last-of-the-breed" heritage, the '53 Chief is surely one of the most collectible of Indians. It represents both the crowning achievement and the sorrowful end of a company that gave generations of motorcyclists some of their fondest memories.

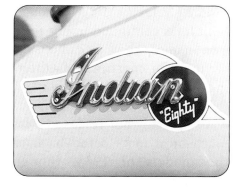

By 1953, the Chief carried acres of sheet-metal, the latest addition being a cowling mounted behind the headlight. Note the running light on the front fender. The rider's view, however, was dominated by chrome. Indian enlarged its 74-cubic-inch V-twin to 80 inches in 1950, and those models received a signifying decal on their fuel tanks.

1954 AJS

In England, during the early 1900s, the Stevens brothers built engines for use in the frames of other manufacturers. In 1909, the initials of the oldest brother, Albert John Stevens, would appear on their first complete motorcycle. AJS built singles and V-twins in the years before World War II, and took home several trophies in the early days of TT racing, which would help sales for many years.

AJS continued as an independent manufacturer until 1931, when financial woes forced it to join forces with the Matchless Company to form Associated Motor Cycles (AMC). Although both lines continued under their own names, they became synonymous in construction, differing only in badging and trim.

The 16M was the first postwar AJS to be released. Its mechanical roots dated back to the models of 1935, though improvements had been implemented in the intervening years. The 16M breathed through larger Amal carbs in 1954, and also had a new automatic ignition-advance mechanism that made riding more pleasant. To make room for this revision, a new side cover was installed, easily identi-

fied by a hump in its surface.

In the postwar era, AJS offered singles and, after 1949, vertical twins. Much like early Fords, AJS cycles of the Fifties were always finished in black, as were their Matchless siblings. However, AJS models wore gold striping, while their Matchless counterparts were trimmed with silver. This was hardly enough to differentiate the two, however, and loyalties to both brands faded.

AMC had purchased ailing Norton in 1952, but resisted the temptation to roll that marque into the same badge-engineering

program as AJS/Matchless—until 1964, that is. First chassis components and then engines were shared, none of which helped sales of any of the makes, and AMC folded in 1966. Matchless was gone for good, but Norton continued under Norton/Villiers, which sold an AJS-badged dirt bike into the mid Seventies.

Though AJS and Matchless machines were virtually identical mechanically, AJS versions had distinct generator-drive covers and wore gold trim rather than silver. Cap-like protrusion in the left-side primary cover ahead of the footpeg housed the new-for-'54 automatic ignition advance. Period AJS/Matchless ad touts the availability of replacement parts, a concern among prospective buyers of foreign machines.

1954 Harley-Davidson FL Hydra-Glide

With the demise of Indian in 1953, Harley-Davidson entered the '54 model year as the sole surviving American motorcycle manufacturer. While that might seem like a cause for celebration in Milwaukee, the truth was that Harley's fortunes were in doubt as well, since bikes from across the pond—particularly England—were becoming as much a threat as Indian ever was.

What the company did celebrate that year was its 50th anniversary. Why this didn't take place the year before (the company having been founded in 1903) is a mystery, but all the '54 models wore special medallions on their front fenders to commemorate the occasion.

The Anniversary Yellow FL shown sports the hand-clutch/foot-shift arrangement introduced in 1952, though traditionalists—and police departments—could still order one with hand shift. Many preferred the older setup because the bike could be left running with the transmission in gear and the clutch disengaged thanks to the "rocking" clutch pedal.

In addition to the commemorative front fender badge, the 50th anniversary FLs were shown with a new trumpet-style horn. This example is fitted with the optional color-matched hand grips and kick-start pedal. Two-tone paint (with the tank and fenders in different colors) was also optional.

FL models accounted for nearly half of all Harleys sold in 1954. Total sales were down from the previous year, and wouldn't rebound until 1957, when the import-fighting Sportster was introduced.

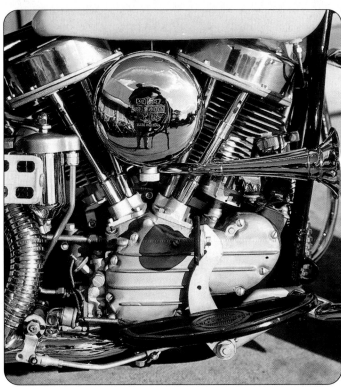

The FL's "Panhead" V-twin displaced 74 cubic inches; the similar EL model, with a 61-cubic-inch engine, was discontinued after 1952. For unknown reasons, Harley-Davidson celebrated its 50th anniversary in 1954, rather than 1953, which would have reflected the company's 1903 founding. Future celebrations would be based on the founding date.

1954 Harley-Davidson FL Hydra-Glide

The big Harleys were always popular with law enforcement. This example is fitted with the "old" hand-shift/foot-clutch arrangement that was still available, largely because it remained popular with police departments. Note the Motorola speaker and microphone by the handlebars; the transceiver was carried in the left saddlebag.

An FL with the optional two-tone paint shows off the also-optional dual exhausts, dual spotlights, and rear luggage carrier. A new trumpet-style horn announced your presence in no uncertain terms.

1956 Simplex Automatic

The Simplex Automatic shown here was designed and built in the U.S. Several other manufacturers used the Simplex name, but they were based in Holland, Italy, and England.

Hailing from New Orleans, Louisiana, the Simplex was the brainchild of Mr. Paul Treen, who started the company in the late Twenties with a $25 investment. A draftsman by trade and inventor by nature, the Simplex was a natural extension of his abilities and vision. Surprisingly, it was the only motorcycle ever built in the southern part of the country.

The first Simplex arrived in 1935, and as the name implied, was built with simplicity in mind. Its 125-cc engine powered the rear wheel through a direct-drive arrangement, eliminating the complexity (and expense) of a transmission and clutch.

Later models, however, added more features. The Simplex Automatic was fitted with an automatic clutch and variable transmission. Furthermore, its two-stroke engine incorporated a rotary valve that was quite unusual for the period. Light weight and efficient design combined to return a claimed 100 mpg.

Fitted with three wheels and a cargo box (similar to Harley-Davidson's larger Servi-Car), the Simplex made a handy around-town runabout. This example is equipped with a tow bar and was popular with service stations, the idea being that it could be towed behind a customer's car being delivered after service work, and then ridden back to the garage.

Simplex cycles were built until 1960. During their life span, revisions were frequent thanks to Mr. Treen's tireless efforts to improve on his simple motorcycle design. The company continued to build go-carts for several years after motorcycle production ceased.

Leading-link front suspension design dated from the earliest days of motorcycling. A single seat spring provided "rear" suspension. Power was routed through an automatic clutch to a variable transmission and then on to the rear wheel. Rather than a chain or plain belt, the Simplex used "linked" belts to transfer driving forces. Evidently, top speed was insufficient to warrant a speedometer.

1957 Ariel 4G Mk II

Ariel was one of the British motorcycle industry's more adventurous manufacturers. Begun in 1902, the company produced an array of singles and twins of both two- and four-stroke design, but it is an unusual four-cylinder model that is perhaps best remembered.

During the 1920s, Ariel's Edward Turner had dreams of changing the world of motorcycling. For many years, twin-cylinder engines were the powerplant of choice, but Turner had grander ideas. Envisioning a four-cylinder engine that would fit neatly into a typical frame, he devised the unusual "square four" design. It used two crankshafts geared together and four cylinders arranged in a square pattern, with a pair of pistons tied to each crankshaft.

Displacing 500 ccs, the first Ariel Square Four appeared in 1931, venting its exhaust through only two pipes. The four was enlarged to 600 ccs in 1932, and then to 1000 ccs in '36. In 1953, the Mk II version appeared, carrying a four-pipe exhaust system and an alloy block in place of the previous iron version.

Some other changes were evident by this time as well. The tank-mounted instrument panel was eliminated and the gauges were now mounted atop the wide headlight nacelle. A new plunger rear suspension provided a softer ride, but needed fresh

Ariel's unique Square Four, sometimes referred to as the "Squariel," originally had only two exhaust pipes exiting the four-cylinder engine, making it look like just a "fat" twin; a four-pipe setup arrived with the Mk II version of 1953. Plunger-type rear suspension design was shared with, among others, Indian. Instruments were originally mounted on top of the fuel tank, but were later moved to the top of the steering head and, in the mid Fifties, to the top of the headlight nacelle, as shown here.

lubrication every 250 miles. The girder front fork had been converted to telescopic in 1946 and went largely untouched.

Turner left Ariel to join Triumph in the mid Thirties, where his talents in developing the Speed Twin (*see* 1947 entry) helped revive the ailing concern. Ariel's success with the Square Four continued through the 1950s, after which the company concentrated on medium-displacement two-strokes that were a cross between a scooter and a motorcycle.

1957 Harley-Davidson XL Sportster

Since the K series introduced in 1952 was getting a lukewarm reception—not to mention regularly beaten by smaller British twins—Harley-Davidson introduced the famed Sportster in 1957. With overhead valves topping a 55-cubic-inch V-twin, the Sportster lived up to its name, proving somewhat quicker than its predecessor.

Save for its overhead-valve engine, the Sportster looked similar to the final KH models—because it was. Telescopic front forks and swingarm rear suspension carried over, as did most styling elements save the two-tone paint treatment and tank badge. Even the engine's primary case looked familiar, the new one differing only in that it had "SPORTSTER" cast into its side.

Like the K-series bikes, Sportsters had their shifters and drive chains on the right, whereas Harley's big FLs had them on the left. In the case of the shifters in particular, this might seem odd, as riders moving up would have to learn to shift with the other foot. But the XL was mimicking British makes, which were its intended target.

Instrument panels held a simple speedometer, while oil pressure and generator warning lights were built into the headlight housing.

Our featured example is painted Pepper Red over black; buyers could request the colors be reversed. Backing the headlight was a cover similar to that used on Harley's big FLs. At first glance, only the cylinder barrels and heads told onlookers this wasn't a KH—well, those and the bold "SPORTSTER" cast into the primary cover.

1958 Cushman Eagle and Pacemaker

Cushman Eagle

Producing its first scooters in the mid 1930s, Cushman went on to build a variety of small machines over the next 30 years. It was one of the few manufacturers of motorized vehicles permitted to continue civilian production during World War II, as its products were considered "energy savers" for those needing transportation to and from work. During this time, and on into the postwar years, many a

Cushman Pacemaker

Eagle's "big bike" mechanical features included telescopic front forks and a hand-shifted two-speed transmission, and it even had dual exhaust pipes. Its Husky engine could be dressed up with a chrome side cover. Pacemaker's sleek "step-through" design made it more popular with women wearing skirts. It retained a leading-link front suspension. Period ad extols the virtues of Cushman-style transportation.

motorcycle enthusiast cut their riding teeth on a Cushman.

Cushman scooters of the Forties were of the "enclosed" variety, with a shroud covering the engine. In 1949, the Eagle was introduced, which copied motorcycle styling themes with its "naked" engine, sprung saddle, contoured fenders, and teardrop fuel tank. Even white-wall tires were available. Its 318-cc flathead single put eight

horsepower through a two-speed transmission, the combination good for 50-plus mph.

Also offered at the time was the Pacemaker, which adhered to conventional scooter lines. Unlike the Eagle, Pacemaker used an automatic clutch and was powered by a smaller engine. Earlier versions had curved, "bathtub" rear bodywork, but 1957 brought a square-cut design intended to look more modern. It met with mixed reviews.

In addition to its two-wheeled scooters, Cushman built other models as well. Often seen putting around golf courses and college campuses were its three-wheeled "pickups," while enclosed versions were popular for parking enforcement.

1958 Harley-Davidson FL Duo-Glide

Finally, after decades of relying only on a sprung saddle for "rear" suspension, the big Harleys adopted a modern swingarm with coil-over shocks in 1958. With that, the Hydra-Glide became the Duo-Glide, upping the ante in the touring market.

Two versions of the Big Twin continued to be offered: The milder, low-compression FL engine ran cooler and was easier to kick over than the hopped-up FLH, making it better suited to around-town driving. Still sized at 1200 ccs/74 cubic inches, period Big Twins were advertised at 53-55 horsepower in the FL, 58-60 in the FLH.

Despite the new rear suspension, a sprung seatpost remained standard, providing what Harley termed "the Glide Ride." Of course, nearly 600 pounds worth of bump-flattening weight didn't hurt, either.

Chrome accessories abounded to put an FL out front in the "see and be seen" sweepstakes. "Be seen" items included chrome crash bars, fender tips, rear grab bar, and instrument panel surround. As far as "seeing" is concerned, well, three headlights should do the trick.

1959 Ariel Leader

Prior to the unveiling of the Leader, Ariel had been best known for its four-stroke singles, twins, and the unique Square Four. But after exhaustive market research, the company decided it was time to change direction.

What appeared in July 1958 was a combination of several new technologies for Ariel, primarily the use of a 250-cc two-stroke engine, pressed-steel frame, and odd-looking trailing-link front forks. The enclosed styling allowed for a chassis structure that stored fuel beneath the seat, while the "tank" served as a convenient storage area.

Another interesting aspect of the Leader was the long list of options available. As a result, few of the 22,000 produced were exactly the same. Color choices included Oriental Blue or Cherry Red with Admiral Gray accents, and the model featured sports the optional side bags and rear luggage rack.

By 1959, Ariel had put all its cards into the Leader, having dropped the Square Four that year. A cheaper, stripped Arrow model followed, as did a Golden Arrow "sport" version. But the deck was stacked against it by this time as Japanese imports flooded the market, and Ariel folded its hand in 1965.

Despite its rather odd looks, the Leader was a functional vehicle that offered many useful features and options. The enclosed body made cleaning a snap, and the full fairing and windshield made cool-weather riding more bearable. Instrument panel included a speedometer, ammeter, and of all things, a clock. Optional luggage rack and side bags add carrying capacity. Note the wild paisley seat cover.

1959 Lilac

While most Fifties imports from Japan were of the scooter variety, Lilacs took a decidedly upmarket approach. Aside from being one of the first "big" Japanese motorcycles sold in the U.S., Lilacs typically sported powertrain layouts resembling those of expensive European bikes.

Starting with simple chain-drive 150-cc four-strokes in the late Forties, Lilac soon converted its line to shaft drive, beginning—oddly—with a little 90-cc single. Success with that model prompted a 350-cc flat twin reminiscent of a BMW, and later a 250-cc transverse V-twin resembling a Moto Guzzi—though interestingly, Lilac's was introduced a good five years before those from Italy.

The combination of a small-displacement V-twin and shaft drive made the Lilac a smooth mount, though not a particularly quick one. Furthermore, the overall design bordered on plain; engine cases and brake drums, for instance, which usually boasted fins or contours on other

Speedometer and warning lights were incorporated into the headlight bucket.

bikes, were smooth-faced and thus devoid of "character."

That's not to say, however, that the Lilac was lacking in style. Front fenders were skirted, seats were plush, and the fuel tank carried trendy chrome panels and rubber knee pads. The Lilac was also equipped with an external tool box and fork-mounted turn signals, along with a speedometer flanked by a trio of warning lights.

A flat twin reappeared in 1964 with 500 ccs of displacement, again shaft driven. But by then, other Japanese manufacturers were flooding the market with less-expensive midsize bikes, and Lilac folded under the competitive pressure after 1969.

Lilac's transverse V-twin preceded those from Moto Guzzi by a good five years, but displaced only 250 ccs. Featureless engine cases were short on character. Shaft drive was a rare feature in '59, as BMW was the only major make to offer it at that time. Turn signals were affixed to the upper fork tubes.

1961 Matchless G-12

The Collier brothers began building motorcycles in 1899, making them one of the oldest British manufacturers on record. Early Matchless machines were assembled using powerplants from a variety of companies, including De Dion, J.A.P., Mag, and MMC, but later models carried engines of the company's own design. In order to prove the abilities of their products, the Collier boys raced their creations, winning the first Isle of Man TT (Tourist Trophy) race in 1907.

With Khaki enamel applied to all fuel tanks in the early years, color was not an option—but a staggering array of available engines were. Offering both side- and overhead-valve powerplants with displacements ranging from 246 ccs up to 990 ccs, buyers could easily tailor a Matchless to suit their needs.

With the industry in a state of turmoil during the early Thirties, Matchless bought out AJS and formed Associated Motor Cycles (AMC). Models continued to be offered under both the Matchless and AJS names, though many were nearly identical in appearance and features.

In the early Forties, Matchless exhibited a rare moment of innovation by bringing out Teledraulic forks, the industry's first telescopic design with oil damping. Soon, they became virtually universal in the motorcycling world.

During World War II, Matchless provided thousands of 350-cc singles to the British military. And in 1952, AMC absorbed Norton.

The 1961 G-12 pictured is a 650-cc vertical twin that competed against similar Triumph and BSA

models of the period, and at least in terms of sales, lost. A larger 750-cc model followed, powered by a Norton vertical-twin engine, but fared little better. AMC restructured in 1966, and afterward, only the Norton name returned to the marketplace.

After Matchless bought out AJS in the early Thirties, both makes continued, but most models were shared between the two lines. The AJS counterpart to this G-12 was called the Model 31, and differed only in that "AJS" badges replaced the "winged M" on fuel tank, side covers, and right-side case covers. Headlight contained a speedometer, ammeter, light switch, and ignition switch.

1961 Velocette Venom

Velocette was founded in 1904 under the name Veloce. Its first motorcycles were powered by four-stroke singles, but when the British company switched to two-strokes in 1913, the name was changed to Velocette. Though four-strokes reappeared in the Twenties, the company name was retained.

When most rivals added large-displacement twins to their line-ups, Velocette stuck with vertical singles. One exception was the LE, introduced in 1949, a small, scooter-like machine powered by a 200-cc horizontally opposed flathead twin. It was a practical mount but never very popular, though Velocette spent plenty trying to make it so.

The single-cylinder Venom was introduced in the late Fifties, and while it was a capable sporting machine, it was overshadowed in the marketplace by various British twins. Its 500-cc engine produced a very respectable 36 horsepower, enough to propel the Venom to near 100 mph. A Venom equipped with the "Clubman" option could top the century mark.

In the mid Sixties the Thruxton Venom appeared, named after a popular racing circuit. But despite an updated appearance and a bit more power, it couldn't save Velocette, and the company folded in 1968.

Velocettes ran with large-displacement singles while most rivals boasted twins. Nonetheless, later models were impressively fast, some able to top 100 mph—though the claim of this mid-Sixties ad that "up to 130 mph can be obtained without muffler" on a 500-cc Thruxton single smacks of hyperbole.

While the left side of the engine was shrouded with black-painted covers, the right side boasted beautiful polished castings. Note the spiffy chrome fuel tank and "fishtail" muffler. Rear suspension could be adjusted to compensate for a passenger's weight by moving the top mounting point of the coil-over shocks—an unusual and useful feature. Bullet headlight housing containing the light switch, ammeter, and speedometer was considered "sleek" in its day.

1963 Harley-Davidson Topper

Capitalizing on the scooter craze then sweeping the country, Harley-Davidson brought out the Topper in 1960. Its 165-cc two-stroke single was started with a recoil starter, like a lawn mower, and drove through a variable-ratio automatic transmission called Scootaway Drive. Up front was a simple leading-link fork, and there were small drum brakes on both wheels. Beneath the hinged seat was a large storage space, but if that wasn't enough, a luggage rack was available.

For those not content with carrying only two people and luggage, a sidecar was offered—though fully loaded, the rig must have proved agonizingly slow. Other "big bike" accessories included a passenger's backrest and windshield.

Despite carrying the revered Harley-Davidson name, the Topper didn't sell particularly well in a market dominated by Japanese machines. And it wasn't long before the scooter craze subsided, taking the Topper as one of its earlier casualties.

A young James Garner tours Hollywood on a Topper.

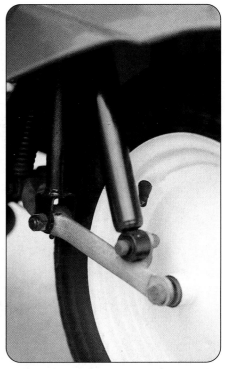

Right-hand side of the leading-link fork carried a simple extension spring behind the pivot point, and a shock absorber in front.

A splashy period brochure entices buyers; inside was a description of the Topper's "high performance" features. The speedometer was difficult for shorter people to see, being situated as it was ahead of and below the handlebars.

1964 Harley-Davidson XL Sportster

After its 1957 introduction, Harley's XL Sportster gained a more sporting version called the XLCH in '59—"CH" supposedly standing for "Competition Hot." These were stripped-down models oriented toward on- and off-road work with magneto ignition, high exhaust pipes, solo seat, smaller "peanut" tank, and lighter overall weight. It also featured the now-famous "eyebrow" headlight cover that remains a Sportster trademark. Harley-Davidson also offered the XLH, a dressed-up, touring-influenced version that was outsold by its sportier sibling.

Power rose steadily over the years, earning the fleet Sportster the nickname "King of the Drags"—an unofficial title it would hold until the late Sixties. Of course, this was at a time when most of its competitors were British 650-cc twins, which spotted considerable displacement to the 883-cc Sportster. And in drag racing, size matters.

Sportster's 883-cc V-twin outpowered most competitors of the era, earning it the nickname "King of the Drags." Since those competitors used right-side shifters, so did the Sportster; Harley's bigger V-twins had their shifters on the left. XLCH introduced the "peanut" tank and "eyebrow" headlight cover that would become Sportster trademarks. Oddly, despite its high-performance aura, it lacked a tachometer, providing only a speedometer. A period Harley ad touts that "Nobody builds a faster stock motorcycle," though the record holders depicted were highly modified machines.

1964 Vespa Allstate Cruisaire

One of the most recognized name in scooters, "Vespa" is actually a model; the parent make is Piaggio of Italy.

Piaggio was established in the late 1800s as an engineering company, eventually expanding to include manufacturing. By the late 1930s it was a sizeable concern involved in numerous endeavors, including aeronautics and ship building. But the company was ravaged during World War II, and afterward looked for a simple product to build that could get it back on its feet.

The need for personal transportation in postwar Italy prompted Piaggio to "think small," and the Vespa scooter was born. Simple and inexpensive, it nonetheless incorporated several interesting features, such as a stamped steel "frameless" chassis that enclosed the 90-cc two-stroke engine, handlebar twist-grip gear change, gear final drive, and single-sided fork and swingarm that allowed easy tire changes. It was an instant hit, and within ten years, more than a million were produced.

So successful was the little scooter that numerous companies outside of Italy sought licenses to produce it. One was Sears, the huge American retailer, which sold it under the Allstate brand.

The 1964 Vespa Allstate pictured differs little from the Italian original, though the engine displaces 125 ccs. Its three-speed transmission is still shifted by

rotating the left handgrip, and the single-sided trailing-link fork and swingarm rear suspension still allow for simple tire changes.

Though Sears no longer offers its Allstate model, Piaggio and the Vespa remains alive and well. Though more futuristic-looking scooters are produced by the Italian concern, a retro version of the original Vespa is a perennial favorite in the company's product line.

Single-sided trailing-link fork allows the tire to be changed by simply removing four wheel nuts. Pulling in the left-hand clutch lever allows the grip to be rotated to select gears. The front brake is actuated by the right handlebar lever, the rear brake by a foot pedal. Kickstart lever sprouts from beneath the right-side engine cover.

1965 BMW R-27

Starting out as a builder of aircraft during World War I, *Bayerische Motoren Werke* turned to motorcycles after the hostilities ceased. Despite the change in products, the company's circular blue-and-white logo—which depicts spinning propeller blades—was retained, and remains to this day.

BMW motorcycles have long been synonymous with horizontal twins and shaft drive, which were used on the very first examples. However, the company also produced smaller single-cylinder machines for many years, and added inline threes and fours in the Eighties.

Early BMWs had stamped-steel frames, and the company was among the first to use telescopic forks starting in 1935. During World War II, Germany purchased thousands of V-twin sidecar-equipped outfits from BMW, and the motorcycle's design prompted the U.S. to commission Harley-Davidson and Indian to build near copies, though only a couple thousand were produced and only a handful saw service.

BMW's first shaft-drive singles arrived in 1925 to satisfy the demand for smaller bikes. Like other BMWs of the day, they used a trailing-link front suspension and rigid frame, switching to telescopic forks in '35 and a plunger rear suspension in '38.

In 1955, BMW replaced its telescopic front end with an Earles fork, which resembles a swing-arm rear suspension in design. In single-cylinder 250-cc form, this model was designated the R-26.

Most mechanical components were carried over from the R-26 to the R-27 shown here. This example has individual "swinging saddles" in lieu of the standard two-up seat, the former supposedly providing more rider and passenger comfort.

Though it grew in popularity throughout its seven-year production run, the R-27 would be dropped after 1967. BMW would not offer another single until the early Nineties, when an Italian-built on/off-road model powered by a Rotax engine was introduced.

Optional rider and passenger "swinging saddles" extended coil springs on impact. BMWs of the era sported Earles-type forks, which provided a very smooth ride; a swingarm pivoted off a rigid fork, with coil-over shocks mounted between the axle and the top of the fork, cushioning bumps. R-27s were occasionally fitted with sidecars, though the bike was somewhat underpowered for this purpose. This one carries the standard one-piece saddle.

1965 DKW Hummel 155

DKW, "*Das Kleine Wunder*" (the little wonder), began assembling powered cycles in 1919, and in 1932 became a partner in the Auto Union conglomerate. Most of DKW's earlier units were built with engines of at least 98 ccs of displacement, but they were always two-stroke designs.

Upon the public introduction of the Hummel 155, the European motoring press dubbed it the "Tin Banana." Its appearance was a radical departure from any contemporary offerings. In addition to the swoopy, avant-garde body work, the Hummel set itself apart from the competition by having a three-speed gearbox. With only a 50-cc engine producing 4.2 horsepower, the 155 was able to cruise at 45 mph. This example is fitted with a conventional foot shifter, though a hand shifter was available as an option.

The art deco styling might have been a big hit in the U.S., but the Hummel was never exported. Being readily available across Europe was not enough to elicit strong demand, and it never sold in great numbers.

Though the Hummel may look whimsical to some, its art-deco styling certainly makes it stand out. Front suspension used an Earles-type fork, much like contemporary BMWs. A "Darth Vader" face shield covers the tiny 50-cc cylinder, while the headlight nacelle redefines the term "streamlined."

1965 Harley-Davidson FL Electra-Glide

For Harley-Davidson, 1965 marked the end of an era. The Electra-Glide, with its electric starter, made its debut, but it would be the last year for the famous "Panhead" V-twin that was introduced in 1948.

That engine had received some modifications over the years, a significant one coming in 1963 with external oil lines that improved lubrication to the cylinder heads. Along with the electric starter came 12-volt electrics to replace the previous 6-volt system, which in turn brought a bigger battery hidden beneath a large battery case on the right side. That, along with the bold "Electra Glide" script on the front fender, makes it easy to distinguish this model from earlier FLs.

The Electra-Glide pictured has the standard ex-

haust system that had both cylinders exhausting to the right into a single muffler; optional was a dual-muffler system where the exhaust from the front cylinder exited to the right, while that from the rear cylinder exited to the left, both terminating in their own distinctive "fishtail" muffler. Also optional was the old hand-shift/foot-clutch arrangement that was so popular with police departments.

Though a curb weight of more than 700 pounds restricted performance somewhat, the Electra-Glide was a popular touring mount in its day, as the electric starter alleviated the problem of having to kick-start the big V-twin—which had become no easy task. And that, combined with being the last model fitted with the venerable Panhead engine, has made it a highly coveted collectible.

The Electra-Glide's mammoth headlight bezel first appeared in 1960, and has become yet another Harley trademark still in use on some models today. Script on the front fender advertised the model's new electric starter, which is mounted at the forward end of the crankcase between the front cylinder and exhaust pipe. Driver's view of the Electra-Glide was dominated by chrome.

1965 Triumph T120 Bonneville

As America's hunger for horsepower grew, Triumph felt the need to supplant its Tiger 110 with a more powerful model. Since Triumph had purebred racing machines streaking across the salt flats of Utah at 150 mph, it was decided to name the new bike after this famous bastian of speed. The Bonneville would be Edward Turner's last Triumph design, and arguably his best.

Introduced in 1959, the Bonneville was powered by Triumph's famous 650-cc twin, but it now inhaled through a pair of Amal carburetors rather than just a sin-

gle carb. While smaller Triumph singles and twins had featured unit construction (engine and transmission in one case) for some time, the 650s had always had them as separate entities, and early Bonnevilles continued this trend. They could easily top the magical 100-mph mark, that imaginary dividing line that separated the men from the boys. As might be expected, the "Bonny" received very favorable reviews and grew into one of Triumph's most popular models.

The 650s were converted to unit construction in 1963, which resulted in a more compact de-

sign; otherwise, this 1965 Bonneville was little changed from the early versions. Today, however, "pre-unit" Triumphs are highly coveted and much sought-after on the collector market.

Popular accessories of the Sixties included the hard Buco panniers (saddle bags). Smiths speedometer read to 120 mph, which the T120 was supposed to be able to achieve—though that was optimistic. Triumph's eggcrate badges and rubber knee pads marked the Bonny's tank.

1966 BSA A65 Spitfire

An ad for the Spitfire plays off famous 1930s-era American bank robbers Bonnie and Clyde, claiming it to be a "Great Getaway Bike."

Like Triumph, BSA's existence revolved around a selection of vertical-twins. But by the mid Sixties the line was glutted with too many variations of the same equipment, so for 1966, BSA reduced its offerings to six models, each with a distinctive profile. Also that year, all BSAs were given 12-volt electrics in place of the outdated 6-volt systems.

The A65 Spitfire was positioned as a road racer for the street. To aid performance, two large-bore Amal GP carburetors were fitted, complete with velo-city stacks. As it turned out, these carbs made the Spitfire difficult to start when hot, and were often replaced with Amal concentrics with round air filters; in light of this, the factory reverted back to the concentric carburetors in '67.

The small two-gallon fuel tank seen on this example was designed for the U.S. market in response to the popularity of the Harley Sportster's "peanut" gas tank. The European Spitfire was equipped with a four-gallon tank, and a five-gallon version was available as an option in 1967.

BSA's 650-cc twins may have been similar in specification to those offered by Triumph, but they didn't look the same; "teardrop" side covers and one-piece rocker covers distinguish the BSA engine. Both Triumph and BSA used Smiths gauges. Note that the tachometer (on right) lacks a redline—a potentially engine-scattering omission.

1966 Harley-Davidson FLH Electra-Glide

In 1965, Harley-Davidson introduced an electric-start version of the big FL series, dubbing it the Electra-Glide. Still powered by the Panhead engine, the big Harley was now carrying not only the additional weight of the inevitable factory- and owner-installed accessories (made more plentiful by a switch from 6-volt electrics to 12), but also the pounds added by the new starting hardware. Though the Panhead had served well during its lengthy tenure, owners were begging for more power.

For 1966, Harley released an updated version of the 74-cubic-inch V-twin. By mating new aluminum "Shovelhead" cylinder heads to the iron barrels, horsepower increased by five: the

FLH now claiming 60, the lower-powered FL 54.

The smoother-running, more powerful Shovelhead engine was a welcome relief. Weight of the FLs had crept up to nearly 800 pounds, and the extra power was appreciated by owners. Yet, despite the greater power and escalating heft, FLs were still slowed by drum brakes front and rear; it wouldn't be until 1972 that a front disc would appear.

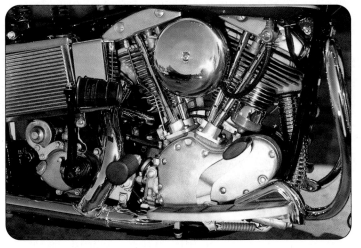

Windshield, dual spotlights, and a backrest for the Buddy Seat were all popular accessories for Harley's big FL, as were the numerous chrome trim pieces. The new Shovelhead engine had valve covers resembling inverted shovel blades, hence the name; it produced about five horsepower more than the outgoing Panhead.

1966 Harley-Davidson Sprint

Introduced in 1961 as a result of a cooperative venture between Harley-Davidson and Aermacchi of Italy, the Sprint was powered by a 250-cc horizontal four-stroke single. Despite being decidedly unlike Harley's traditional products of the time, the Sprint was quite popular with buyers.

Little had changed by 1966, when this example was built, though styling had become somewhat more modern. Both street and on/off-road Scrambler models were offered by that time, and modified versions enjoyed a fair degree of competition success.

Displacement increased to 350 ccs for 1969 on the street-going Sprint—now called the SS—while the Scrambler version did not get the larger engine until 1972. Both models disappeared after 1974 to be replaced by two-stroke machines, also built by Aermacchi.

A Harley ad of the period asked, "Would you like to quarterback 250cc of hustle?"

The crankcase cover may have read "Harley-Davidson," but the overhead-cam single was built by Aermacchi of Italy, and like the Sportster, came with a right-side shifter. It was surprisingly potent in competition; Harley's CR250 flat-tracker was a competitive mount right out of the box.

1966 Suzuki T10

The Suzuki we know today started out in 1909 building an entirely different sort of machine. Silk production was a major industry in Japan at the time, and the company got its start making silk looms.

Though Suzuki built an experimental engine in the late Thirties with an eye toward production, World War II intervened. After the war, the company switched to heaters and farm machinery, and it wasn't until 1952 that the engine resurfaced. This came in the form of a small 36-cc two-stroke that could be fitted to a bicycle, and Suzuki was on the road.

Production of a complete 90-cc motorbike began in 1954, and Suzuki was one of the first companies to introduce oil injection on its two-strokes, which

relieved riders of having to mix the gas and oil themselves. In 1963, Suzuki built a road-going version of a 250-cc two-stroke twin that had been raced in the Fifties, calling it the T10.

Along with oil injection, the T10 was fitted with such luxuries as electric start, hydraulic rear brake, turn signals (not yet universal), and an enclosed drive chain. Its pressed-steel frame resulted in flowing contours aft of the chrome-sided fuel tank, and that, along with 17-inch wheels, tire-hugging front fender, and telescopic front forks, gave the T10 a contemporary look. Performance was not a priority, the T10 being aimed at commuters with its mild-mannered engine boasting a broad torque range. That philosophy, however, was about to change.

Twin-cylinder two-stroke featured oil injection, an unusual convenience at the time. Aimed more at luxury than performance, the T10 included only a speedometer in its headlight-mounted instrument panel. Suzuki made a point in advertising that the odd-shaped headlight was brighter than most, aiding nighttime safety. An enclosed drive chain helped keep the bike—and the rider—free from messy chain-lube splatters.

1967 Bridgestone 350 GTO

While the name "Bridgestone" is associated with tires today, during the Sixties it was synonymous with "performance" in motorcycle circles—though that really wasn't the company's original aim.

When Honda began enjoying success in the U.S. with 50-cc scooters, Bridgestone jumped on the bandwagon with a similar model originally sold through Sears and Montgomery Wards stores. The company then expanded into true motorcycles, the first being a hot 175-cc two-stroke twin that could embarrass many 350s. Then Bridgestone came out with a 350 of its own, which could likewise dust bikes twice its size.

Introduced in the mid Sixties, the 350 GTR used racing-technology rotary disc valves in the crankcase to help get 40 horsepower from a mere 21 cubic inches. That, combined with light weight and a 6-speed transmission, allowed the GTR to turn high 13s in the quarter-mile when most British 650 twins were running mid 14s.

A "scrambler" version of the GTR followed, earning its on/off-road status with little more than a high-mounted exhaust pipe—which hardly a true scrambler made. And though the new GTO shared the GTR's virtues, few were sold, making our featured model rare indeed.

For reasons that have never been explained, Bridgestone suddenly halted motorcycle production in the late Sixties. Some rumors had it that other Japanese motorcycle manufacturers, which purchased millions of tires from Bridgestone, convinced the company that its continued efforts at building competing bikes might jeopardize its much-more-profitable tire business. But whatever the reason, Bridgestone motorcycles were never to be again.

Twin rotary valves helped give the 350-cc twin prodigious power for its size. Just above the footpeg bolt is a splined shaft exiting the crankcase cover; it's an extension of the shift-lever shaft, and allows riders to switch the shift lever to the right side of the bike if desired to match the British format. "Kickup" at the rear of the seat was a Bridgestone signature. Behind the turn signal, just above the exhaust pipe, is the tool box—a great place to keep a hot dog warm. Tachometer on right shows an 8000-rpm redline; not particularly high considering the power output.

1967 Triumph T100C Tiger

Throughout the Fifties and Sixties, Triumph sold a complete line of small and midsize motorcycles aimed at the first-time rider. One of the most popular was the Tiger 100, which was introduced in 1960 as the T100A. A vertical twin of 500 cc displacement, it wore two-tone paint and "bathtub" tank badges.

In 1966, the Tiger received a thorough makeover. A new frame combined with better forks improved handling and stability. Two-tone paint continued, but tank badges were changed to a new "eyebrow" style.

Offered alongside the T100A touring model was the T100C, an on/off-road bike that sported a smaller fuel tank and headlight, along with high-mounted twin exhaust pipes. A skidplate was added to protect the underside of the engine during off-road excursions, and an alternator replaced the old Energy Transfer electric system. U.S. versions received alloy fenders in place of the steel units found on their European counterparts.

T100 models continued to be popular right into the Seventies, when in 1973 the T100C was reborn as the TR5T Trophy Trail.

Tiger's 500-cc twin looked similar to Triumph's 650-cc engine, though the latter had larger cooling fins on the head and added fins on the rocker covers. "Eyebrow" tank badges were adopted in 1966. Tiger engine was fed by a single carb and was thus much easier to keep in tune than the twin-carb setup on the sportier 500-cc Daytona, introduced in 1967. As on many other Triumphs of the era, the engine's redline was anybody's guess.

1969 BSA Rocket 3

BSA earned its reputation with four-stroke singles and twins, but in 1968, the company broke with tradition and introduced the three-cylinder Rocket 3. Nearly a clone of the Triumph Trident, the Rocket II was powered by an alloy 750-cc overhead-valve engine producing 58 horsepower—enough to propel the bike to near 120 mph. Later models would have even more power and higher top speeds. In 1971, a Rocket 3 was ridden to victory at the Daytona 200, but that would prove to be a farewell appearance.

Had the Rocket 3 been introduced three or four years earlier as originally planned, its impact would have been extraordinary. But by 1969, the Rocket 3's contemporary styling and ample power were not enough to fend off the stampede of new large-displacement motorcycles that began coming out

of Japan that year, most notably the Honda 750 Four. As such, its life was short, and it didn't prove to be the savior BSA had hoped for—and needed.

Though mechanically similar to the Triumph Trident introduced the same year, the Rocket 3 looked decidedly different with its canted cylinders, painted fenders, and "ray gun" mufflers with their trio of protruding pipes. Traditional Smiths gauges provided a clean look from the rider's seat. The potent 750-cc triple produced 58 horsepower; the center cylinder's exhaust pipe split in two and each branch joined with an outside pipe. Later models, with a bit more power and taller gearing, could pull the speedometer needle to 130. Per common English practice, the redline was omitted.

1969 Honda CB750

In June of 1968, Honda dropped the gauntlet that would forever change the world of motorcycling. The CB750/4 offered a combination of hardware never before seen on a single machine.

At the heart of the CB750 was an inline four-cylinder engine with single overhead cam, four carburetors, prominent four-into-four exhaust, and 67 horsepower at 8000 rpm. For those keeping track, it put out a good 15-percent more power than BSA's new 750-cc Rocket 3 and at just under 500 pounds, weighed about the same. It's not hard to guess which was quicker.

But it wasn't just the four-cylinder engine that caused such a stir; though most contemporary competitors were twins, fours had been offered by several manufacturers in the past. No, it was the fact that

four-cylinder power and smoothness was joined by a five-speed gearbox, electric starter, and a front disc brake—the first ever on a street machine—all at a reasonable price.

The first CB750s were produced with sand-cast cases that had a rough finish; later models had smoother castings. Those early sand-cast models, such as the bike pictured, have become the most valuable to collectors.

By 1970, Dick Mann had piloted a race-prepped CB750 into the winner's circle at Daytona, and the world of aftermarket hop-up equipment came alive. The CB750 is also credited with casting the mold for what would later be called the "Universal Japanese Motorcycle," a breed of machines that would bring the bikes of England to their collective knees.

With 67 horsepower at 8000 rpm, the CB750's four-cylinder engine was both powerful and smooth. Redline was 8500 rpm. For the first time on a production bike, a front disc brake was standard equipment; fitting, given the whopping speed potential, which was claimed to be 130 mph.

1969 Honda Dream 305

Soichiro Honda's first effort, the 98-cc two-stroke Model D of 1947, was considered quite rough when compared to its competition. Since then, however, the company that bears his name has undergone some radical changes.

After years of development and growth, Honda found itself flirting with bankruptcy in 1953. But it managed to hang on, and in 1958, the C100 Super Cub was introduced. Powered by a 50-cc four-stroke single, it was an instant hit. The Cub's light weight and step-through design appealed to a large audience, and by 1960, Honda was shipping more than 169,000 units per year to 50 countries around the globe.

The Dream 305 followed in its footsteps, and was likewise enjoying robust sales by the mid Sixties. Like its forbearer, it was light and easy to handle; but with its 305-cc overhead-cam twin-cylinder engine, it was far more powerful, with a top speed of near 100 mph. Furthermore, it could be dressed up with a dizzying array of saddlebags, luggage racks, and windscreens to increase its usefulness and individualize its personality.

Amazingly, its production run would last ten years. By the late Sixties, consumer interest was moving toward larger, more powerful motorcycles, and Honda replaced the Dream with larger twins and the formidable 750 four.

Stamped-steel forks hid the inner workings of the leading-link front suspension. Gear-shift lever had both toe and heel pads for easy shifting of the four-speed transmission. Instrumentation was sparse, but the Dream could nearly bury the needle of the 100-mph speedometer. Stamped-steel mufflers showed a prominent seam along the edges.

1970 BSA Lightning

BSA recorded record profits heading into the Sixties, but by the time the 1970 models hit showroom floors, the company was struggling to keep its head above water. The reason, of course, was the cheaper—and often faster—Japanese motorcycles such as the Honda 750 Four, Yamaha 650 twin, and various Kawasaki and Suzuki large-displacement two-strokes.

Due to its proven track record, the 650-cc vertical twin used in the Lightning was also the powerplant of choice for several other BSA models. But because funds were beginning to dry up, the company made few product changes in 1970, though one model, the Royal Star, was dropped due to slow sales.

Among those few changes were better brakes for the Lightning, which now sported an eight-inch drum with twin leading shoes up front, and a seven-inch drum in back. Also, a passenger grab rail was added that surrounded the rear section of the seat. For 1971, the oil tank beneath the seat was deleted, as the hollow tubes of the frame itself were now used to hold the oil.

BSA didn't survive long afterward, however, as the competition from Japan proved too much for the beleaguered company. BSA was folded into Norton-Villiers in 1973, which spelled the end of the BSA nameplate, though Triumph (which BSA had acquired in the early '50s) continued to scrape along for another decade or so before the whole empire collapsed.

A 1966 ad for the Lightning boasts that it was the "fastest motorcycle ever tested by HOT ROD magazine," a claim that would prove to be short-lived.

For 1970, the Lightning gained an eight-inch, twin-leading-shoe front brake with a racing-style air scoop on the right side. Also new was the passenger grab rail that surrounded the rear section of the seat. This would be the last of BSA's twins to have an oil tank beneath the seat; starting in 1971, the oil was carried in the frame tubes.

1970 Ducati 350 Scrambler

Starting out as an electronics firm in the mid Twenties, Ducati lost everything in World War II and had to rebuild. As in many other countries, Italy was in need of personal transport, so the company began producing a small engine that could be mounted on a bicycle. However, it differed from most others of its kind in being a four stroke with integral two-speed transmission.

By the early Fifties, Ducati was building complete motorcycles, though only small, pedestrian ones. This changed in 1955 when a 98-cc single appeared with bevel-driven overhead cam, a layout that would define Ducati engines for the next few decades. It was instantly successful in racing, and led to larger and more powerful machines.

Another Ducati trademark was desmodromic valve actuation, which was introduced on a 125-cc racer in 1956. Instead of using springs to close the valves, which often "floated" at high rpm, they were closed mechanically. This feature didn't show up on production models until the late Sixties, but these 250- and 350-cc singles were quick bikes indeed, and a 450 that followed was even quicker. However, only the sporting Ducatis got the "desmo" valve-train; tamer models used valve springs.

The 350 Scrambler featured here was considered one of the "tamer" models, though it was still fast for a bike of its size. Singles lasted until 1973, by which time the V-twins introduced two years earlier had taken over the showrooms.

Though the Scrambler didn't carry Ducati's famed desmodromic valvetrain, like all Ducati four-strokes of the period, it did have bevel-gear cam drive; one of the gears is evident inside the black ring at the top of the engine. As with many other bikes of the era, the Scrambler's speedometer was mounted in the headlight housing, though the needle's direction of travel was reversed from common practice.

1970 Norton Commando 750S

Norton was one of the first British motorcycle manufacturers, having offered what was essentially a bicycle with an engine attached as early as 1902. Larger machines followed, most powered by proprietary engines built by Peugeot of France.

The Norton name is steeped in racing history, the company winning its first contest in 1907. A dizzying array of motorcycles followed: large, small, two-stroke, four-stroke, some with engines made by Norton, some with proprietary units. By the Twenties, however, most were powered by large Norton-built four-stroke singles, and racing victories continued.

It wasn't until after World War II that Norton ventured into vertical twins. The first was the Dominator, whose 500-cc overhead-valve twin would form the basis for Norton's big bikes for many years to come.

In 1953, with finances tight, Norton became part of Associated Motor Cycles (AMC), where it joined AJS and Matchless. Two years later, Nortons went on sale in the U.S. for the first time, where its 500-, 650-, and later 750-cc twins gained a strong reputation for power and handling.

A Norton ad insists that "she's just about the most beautiful thing you have seen on two wheels." They're talking about the bike, of course....

In an attempt to recapture some of the customers escaping to other machines, Norton created the Commando for 1968. By combining a strong frame, 750-cc vertical-twin engine, and rubber mounting points, the Isolastic System was born. By reducing vibration, it was hoped that this model could successfully battle the newcomers from Japan.

Aside from the Isolastic System, much of the Commando's hardware was common to other Norton models. At the front end, Roadholder forks were lengthened and held eight-inch, twin-leading-shoe brakes. Out back, the Girling shocks could be adjusted to one of three settings to optimize comfort and handling. The time-tested vertical-twin engine featured cylinder heads, push rods, and connecting rods made of aluminum.

The Commando appeared in several configurations during its lifetime, and the "S" model first arrived in 1969. Its distinctive high exhaust pipes with heat shields set the S apart from other Commandos. More importantly, the S stood for Sport, and magazine reviews raved about the new levels of performance. But despite its 125-mph capabilities, the S model slipped into oblivion during the 1970 model year, though the Commando line itself continued on into the mid Seventies.

1970 Triumph Tiger 650

Throughout the 1960s, England found its economy slipping into a sea of red ink. Many large companies were closing their doors and unemployment was rampant. As a method of keeping some of these firms afloat, the government offered infusions of cash as long as the firm would also take on engineers from the bloated military pool. Although the capital was a welcome relief, engineers that were hired by various motorcycle manufacturers thought like engineers rather than motorcycle enthusiasts, and many of the changes that came about were questionable at best.

Triumph had offered a wide variety of machines throughout its history, but vertical twins, starting with the 500-cc Speed Twin of 1937, soon became the most popular. By the Fifties, the engine had grown to 650 ccs as found in the Thunderbird, and later the Bonneville and Tiger models.

Both the Bonneville and Tiger were fitted with the same basic powerplant, but the latter had only one carburetor, trading a bit of horsepower for easier starting, better fuel economy, and less fussy operation. As a result, the Tiger wasn't quite as quick as the Bonneville, but was considered to be a better all-around choice for many riders.

Bonneville and Tiger grew to 750 ccs for the 1973 model year and were soon joined by the three-cylinder Trident. But their days were numbered; the Japanese, with their more advanced machines, were about to take over.

Tiger was the single-carb stablemate of the more famous Bonneville. Though the latter was faster, its Amal carburetors were renowned for going out of sync, which made the engine run poorly. With its lone carburetor, the Tiger was easier to keep in tune. Like the Bonneville, it carried a ventilated front drum brake and Smiths gauges.

1971 Harley-Davidson FX Super Glide

In an effort to compete head-on with the aftermarket suppliers, Harley-Davidson ushered in its first "factory custom" for the 1971 model year. By combining pieces from two popular models, the "Big Twin" FL and the XL Sportster, the company hoped to provide buyers a new breed of Harley.

Stripped of its electric starter, the FX could be fitted with a smaller battery and battery box. The forks and front wheel were taken from the XL's parts bin, as was a smaller-diameter headlight and trademark headlight cover. The frame, 74-cubic-inch Shovelhead engine, and rear suspension originated from the FL. The dual tanks were from the

FLH. A fiberglass tail section was styled after a similar piece used on the previous year's Sportster, and all the bodywork could be covered with a special Sparkling America paint scheme.

New and exciting as it was, the market failed to respond to the first Super Glide, and only 4700 found buyers. By comparison, over 10,000 Sportsters were sold the same year.

The Super Glide returned for 1972, but some of its pieces did not. The tail section disappeared, replaced by a traditional steel fender assembly. In this form, the Super Glide met with greater success, and factory customs would eventually become Harley-Davidson's stock-in-trade.

Although Harley's first factory custom didn't go over very well, many who turned it down no doubt regret their decision today. "Boat tail" rear fender was styled after the one that appeared on the 1970 Sportster—where it didn't meet with overwhelming approval, either—but while the two looked similar, they were not interchangeable. Sportster forks, with their trademark "eyebrow" casting over the headlight and fork brace below it, lent the big Super Glide a lighter, dragster-like look.

1971 Munch TTS

Embracing the philosophy that "bigger is better," Friedl Munch of Germany introduced the bike that bears his name in 1966. At a time when it was rare that a motorcycle was larger than 750 ccs (Harleys excluded, of course), the first Munch carried a 1000-cc four-cylinder NSU automotive powerplant—and they would get even bigger. By the time production wound down in the 1980s, displacement was up to 1286 ccs, resulting in 104 fuel-injected horsepower.

Only about 250 Munch motorcycles were ever built, with fewer than 50 delivered to the United States. It's rumored that no two were exactly alike. Styling can best be described as bulky, weight the same. The TTS shown is powered by a 1200-cc four, and carries dual headlights (a Munch trademark), "turbine vane" cast rear wheel, spoke front wheel with huge drum brake, and a full complement of gauges, including a clock.

1972 Kawasaki H2 750 Mach IV

Founded in the late 1800s, Kawasaki has been into everything from planes to trains to shipping. Though it supplied small motorcycle engines (complete with transmissions) to other manufacturers since just after World War II, Kawasaki did not offer its own bikes until 1960. But this new segment of the company advanced—and grew—quickly.

One of the manufacturers using those small engines was Meguro, which Kawasaki bought out in the early Sixties. The first machines that wore Kawasaki badges were 125-cc commuter bikes, which didn't go over well when the company exported them to the United States. But Meguro had also been building a 650-cc four-stroke overhead-valve twin under license from BSA (the English company's old pre-unit model), and this met with a fair degree of success in the U.S. when introduced as the W1 in 1966. But better—and faster—models were yet to come.

First up was a 250-cc two-stroke twin called the Samurai, which certainly represented an about-face

in philosophy from the W1. Fitted with rotary disc valves, it was a hot little number, and the temperature was raised further by the 350-cc Avenger that followed. And then came the big one.

In the midst of numerous new "superbikes" being introduced by Triumph, BSA, and Honda, the 500-cc H1 Mach III two-stroke triple stood out as a ferocious performer at a cut-rate price. Light and very powerful, with 60 horses that seemed to lie in wait and then suddenly stampede when the revs built up, rumors abounded of Mach IIIs that reared up and threw their riders off on the first test drives. But in the raging superbike wars, "too much" was still not enough.

Enter the 750-cc H2 Mach IV. With 74 horsepower on tap, it was even more fearsome than the Mach III. And not surprisingly, it inherited several of its parent's flaws, namely squirrely handling, a propensity to wheelie, and horrific fuel mileage. So although it was perhaps the ultimate performance two-stroke of the day, the market—and Kawasaki—would soon be drifting toward more civilized four-strokes.

Peaky power output of the Mach IV's 750-cc triple often proved troublesome for the unwary. Big front disc was reassuring given the bike's 130-mph speed potential, but did little good when the front wheel was in the air. Three-pipe exhaust system mounted two pipes on one side, one on the other.

1973 Kawasaki Z-1

After Honda introduced the CB750 in 1969, other Japanese manufacturers scrambled to best the effort. One of the most notable outcomes of this mad dash was Kawasaki's Z-1.

Kawasaki had made its mark in the U.S. with its fast but frightening two-stroke triples, but Honda's success with its more civilized CB 750 Four did not go unnoticed. The market was beginning to lean away from two-strokes in general, and Kawasaki wanted to maintain its performance image while offering a more roadable four-stroke machine.

Introduced in 1973, the Z-1 boasted a 903-cc double-overhead-cam inline four that significantly upped the performance ante. That engine soon became the benchmark other companies would aim to beat, and it proved to be a bulletproof design that continues to be a dominant force in racing circles to this day.

In contrast to the strong-running powerplant, the chassis of the Z-1 was notoriously unstable. Several aftermarket manufacturers quickly devised more competent frame designs that could be filled with Z-1 power.

No color options were offered for the U.S. market, all Z-1s being painted brown with orange accents. Not considered a particularly appealing combination at the time, many early Z-1s received custom paint treatments shortly after leaving the showroom.

Kawasaki wanted to trump Honda's hand, and did so with a state-of-the-art 900-cc double-overhead-cam four producing 82 horsepower—15 more than the Honda—that could rev to a stratospheric (for the time) 9000 rpm. It was also decidedly more docile and forgiving than Kawasaki's earlier two-stroke machines. Kawasaki called it "the ultimate way to come out ahead…."

1973 Moto Guzzi V7 Sport

Moto Guzzi began building motorcycles in 1920, becoming known for its horizontal single-cylinder engines with the cylinder pointing straight out toward the front wheel. Surprisingly, this design carried on for more than 45 years with only minor changes.

Most of these singles displaced about 500 ccs, and though many Moto Guzzis had a sporting nature, none were really fast. During that same time period, however, the company produced some racing machines that were very technically advanced, inclu-

ding supercharged triples and, in the mid Fifties, a magnificent V-8.

It wasn't until the mid 1960s that Moto Guzzi replaced the horizontal single with its now-famous V-twin. Mounted in a bike called the V7, this engine initially displaced 700 ccs, but was bumped to 750 ccs in 1969.

The V7 used shaft drive in place of a chain, and when fitted with the proper accessories, made for an impressive touring mount. But in an effort to reach a more sporting audience, Moto Guzzi rolled out a trimmed-down version that was called—appro-

priately—the V7 Sport.

Early models, such as the example shown here, had a silver-painted chassis, though later models switched to basic black. All Moto Guzzis got a new frame and a front-mounted alternator in 1972, which allowed for a lower seat height; in the case of the V7 Sport, it measured only 29½ inches off the ground. When combined with the Sport's relatively flat handlebars, it resulted in a low riding position and low center of gravity, which helped the V7 Sport hold true to its name.

Low-set handlebars, huge front drum brake—and, of course, the "Sport" nomenclature—mark this V7's intentions.
As can be seen in this 1968 ad, the original V7, from which the Sport was derived, was aimed more at the touring market.

1974 Laverda SFC

Laverda grew out of an Italian agricultural-machinery company that had been established in the late 1800s. The first motorcycle, a little 75-cc single built in 1948, was really more of "hobby" bike than a prototype, but people liked it and the company elected to go into full-scale production.

Though some Laverdas enjoyed a fair degree of racing success, they were mostly small-displacement machines, and the company's civilian offerings were decidedly on the pedestrian side. But that changed quickly in the mid 1960s.

Though the 650-cc twin that appeared in 1966 was hardly a space-age design, it did boast a single overhead cam when most British rivals were still using overhead-valve layouts. Quite quick for its day, it also had electric start (something the Brits wouldn't adopt until much later), and was a quality piece of work.

The 650 soon grew to 750 ccs, and sportier versions appeared. Leading the performance pack was the SFC, with a high state of tune that produced 70 horsepower, along with pared-down bodywork, a sleek fairing, and triple disc brakes. As such, it was really a racer for the street, and in fact did very well in competition. Soon, however, the 750 would grow again, and not just in displacement.

Racing-style saddle left little (actually, no) room for a passenger. Huge Brembo disc brakes (two in front, one in the rear) were of competition caliber. The 750 twin pushed out 70 horsepower; by contrast, the Honda 750 four made only 67 and could happily spin past 8000 rpm—which wasn't recommended on the Laverda.

1974 MV Agusta 750 GT

Having its roots in aviation is only fitting for one of Italy's most respected racing marques. During its heyday, MV Agusta claimed 37 Manufacturer's World Championships, and its fleet flyers occupied the winners circle at the end of 270 Gran Prix races.

After World War II, MV turned its attention from airplanes and helicopters to small motorbikes, which were in great demand throughout Europe. But it was racing that most interested the company, and MV duly entered competition with a 500-cc four-cylinder machine in the early Fifties. Success with that and smaller racers followed, though MV's street bikes of the period were smaller singles and twins.

That changed in 1965 with the introduction of a 600-cc four-cylinder road bike. Fours weren't at all common at that time, but this one was nothing special in the performance department thanks to high

weight, a mild state of tune, and shaft drive—the last a bit of a detriment because it forces the power flow to take a 90-degree turn, which saps some of the energy. Nevertheless, MV fours would retain shaft drive for the next 15 years.

In the late Sixties, MV brought out the 750 Sport, which (as the name implied) was a performance-oriented machine more in keeping with the company's racing heritage. This double-overhead-cam engine was later bumped up to 790 ccs (though the bikes still wore "750" markings) the change boosting horsepower from 69 to 75.

The 750 GT was aimed at both performance and luxury, being fitted with high handlebars, a large fuel tank, and diamond-quilted seat. But like all MV Agustas, it remained extremely expensive, especially compared to the Japanese fours that were by that time dominating the market, and relatively few were sold.

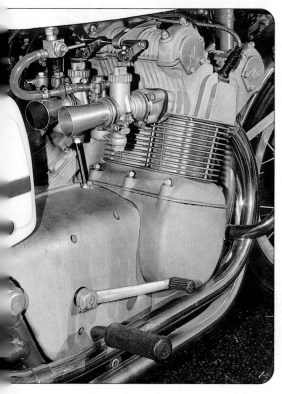

Bulky, square-edged fuel tank and unpolished engine cases seemed at odds with the MV's lofty price, but closer inspection reveals a high level of quality. Dash panel was more ornate than most. Shaft drive was unusual for a high-performance inline-four in the mid Seventies, as was the front drum brake—however large it might be.

1974 MZ TS250

As seldom as they are seen here in the states, MZs are popular overseas, as the company was the leading builder of motorcycles in Eastern Europe for many years. Not only were MZs popular with the masses, they were also accomplished in several arenas of racing, including trials and road circuits. Mike Hailwood rode a factory MZ race bike before his stint with Ducati.

First built in Zschopau, East Germany, the MZ TS250 is about what you would expect from the former Communist country. Looking at its street machine, it would be hard to guess that the company had any racing blood in its veins. Powered by a simple 250-cc two-stroke single, the TS250 is not about to set any speed records.

Though silver paint substitutes for chrome plating on the fenders, the bulbous fuel tank is dressed to kill with its chrome side panels. Chrome plating is also found on the large headlight nacelle.

Suspended with common underpinnings and slowed with nothing more than drum brakes, the MZ is a basic mount, but in the mid Seventies, it dutifully filled its homeland's need for simple transportation.

Long forks, small front wheel, and boxy fuel tank give the TS250 an awkward stance. Note that the mirror is attached to the end of the left handlebar. Oddly, the mirror and fenders are painted silver, while the tank side panel, air-cleaner cover, and headlight are chromed. Single-cylinder two-stroke is no road burner, but isn't meant to be. Gas cap heralds the company's string of victories in the International Six Days trials event.

1974 Yamaha RD350

Originally a manufacturer of musical instruments, Nippon Gakki added a small motorcycle to its line after World War II. It was based on the same German DKW 125-cc two-stroke single as the postwar BSA Bantam and Harley-Davidson S-125, and like those models, proved successful in the postwar seller's boom. In honor of Nippon's founder, it was given the name "Yamaha."

Yamahas were reasonably successful in racing during the Fifties, and when the company bought Showa late in the decade, it added that firm's knowledge of rotary valves to its engineering portfolio. Following were a series of larger twins up to 305 ccs, all two-strokes. The largest eventually evolved into the 350-cc RD series of 1973.

By that time, Yamaha had already branched out into four-stroke twins represented by the 650-cc XS1, and though variations of that model would continue for a good many years, the company didn't abandon two-strokes—at least, not yet.

The RD350 was a landmark bike, being light and very powerful for its size. Thanks to reed-valve induction, it had a broader power band than most two-strokes, making it easier to ride in traffic. Smaller versions with as little as 125 ccs followed, and the 350 grew to 400 ccs in 1976. But two-stroke street bikes in general were not long for this world, as they were being squeezed out by U.S. emission laws, and the RD series was discontinued in 1980.

Powerful two-stroke twin made the lightweight RD350 a quick bike for its size, yet reed-valve induction (what Yamaha marketed as "Torque Induction)" also made it docile in traffic. Redline was 8500 rpm. The speed potential of the RD made the front disc brake a welcome feature.

1975 Harley-Davidson SS-250

Harley-Davidson had formed a partnership with Aermacchi of Italy in the early Sixties to sell midsize four-stroke singles under the H-D badge. These were soon joined by a host of two-stroke models as small as 65 ccs, and even some minibikes. But while the larger singles were fairly successful, the times prompted something a bit more modern.

One of a quartet of new midsize two-stroke singles based on a Yamaha design and introduced by Harley-Davidson in the mid Seventies, the SS-250 appeared in 1975 and was the largest street version offered. On/off-road models carried the SX prefix, and both bikes were eventually available in 175- and 250-cc sizes.

However, the Environmental Protection Agency was beginning to frown on all two-stroke bikes as a major source of pollution. As a result, the switch to two-strokes was—in retrospect—perhaps not the best choice, and Harley-Davidson quit offering singles of any type after 1978.

Yamaha-based engine provided decent performance, but its emissions eventually ran afoul of the EPA. Like most Harleys of the era, fuel tanks carried the AMF logo (the sporting-goods manufacturer had purchased Harley-Davidson in 1969) and corporate tri-color striping theme. Though American colors and the Harley logo appeared prominently on the bike, many purists felt it was a Harley-Davidson in name only. A Harley-Davidson ad touts the SS-250 as a bike "For the discriminating road and highway rider."

1975 Honda CB400

After introducing the world to "popularly priced" four-cylinder motorcycles with the CB750 in 1969, Honda followed with a string of lighter fours featuring engines as small as 350 ccs. One of the most sporting of these was the CB400, introduced in 1975.

For the most part, the CB400 was simply an upgraded version of the 350 model from the previous year. The most striking change was the swoopy four-into-one exhaust system that snaked around the frame, converging into a single muffler on the right side of the bike. Also noticeable were the angular fuel tank and flat cafe-style handlebars, all of which gave the bike a more racer-like look and feel than the rather pedestrian 350.

Although aimed at the sporting segment of the market, the CB400 came up a little short in the performance department compared to the competition, most notably the quick but noisy two-stroke triples from Kawasaki. But whatever the CB400's engine lacked in power it made up for in refinement, the small-displacement four-stroke being smooth and less audibly irritating than a two-stroke. To help keep the engine in its power band, Honda employed a six-speed transmission—something of a rarity at the time.

The CB400 could out-handle most sporting machines of the era, though it couldn't keep up on the straights. The 408 cc inline four with its tangle of four-into-one exhaust pipes was backed by a six-speed transmission, which helped keep the high-winding engine in its power band; redline was a lofty 10,000 rpm. Front disc brake provided great stopping power to the lightweight machine.

1975 Honda GL1000 Gold Wing

After showing the world what it could do with the CB 750 in 1969, Honda was ready to do it again in '75. When the GL 1000 Gold Wing arrived that year, it was obvious Honda had become a leader in motorcycle technology.

Besides the unusual water-cooled "flat four" engine that displaced 999 ccs, the GL 1000 came equipped with shaft drive. The "fuel tank" was nothing more than a cover for the electronics; the real tank was located between the two side covers for a lower center of gravity.

The price to be paid for all these features was weight, as a bare-bones version tipped the scales at a hefty 584 pounds. And being a touring mount, most riders added a fairing, saddlebags, luggage carrier, and other options that hiked the total up even further.

In the first five years of production, Honda sold just under 100,000 copies of a motorcycle that would become a legend. The original Gold Wing has since grown into a six-cylinder, 1500-cc behemoth that comes complete with a reverse gear and more electronic amenities than the space shuttle.

An early Gold Wing ad contained little besides glowing reports from various motorcycle magazines.

Honda's Gold Wing did to the touring market what the CB750 had done to the performance market several years earlier. Rarely was a Gold Wing seen *au naturel* as shown here; they were usually loaded down with fairings, bags, and travel trunks. By that time, they typically weighed in at close to 700 pounds, so the torquey 1000-cc overhead-cam flat-four engine and triple disc brakes were much appreciated by riders. Shaft drive was rare at the time, but its reliability and clean-running characteristics made it perfect for touring duty.

1975 Suzuki GT 750

Long a producer of small- and medium-displacement two-stroke street bikes, Suzuki went out on a technological limb in 1971 and introduced the GT750. It became known as the "Water Buffalo" due to its large-displacement water-cooled two-stroke engine.

Two-strokes had been used on and off since the turn of the century, but were usually singles or twins of 250 ccs or less. Suzuki brought out the Titan in the mid Sixties, a 500-cc twin that was probably the largest two-stroke street bike to achieve any kind of popularity up to that time. Racing motorcycles were the usual recipients of two-strokes due to their light weight and high, but narrow, power band.

Being water cooled, the GT750 had a sizable radiator bolted to the front chassis downtubes. The engine's water jacket kept it cool and helped to reduce noise. The three-cylinder engine dumped its spent exhaust into four separate pipes, each with a full-length megaphone that was made up of two halves joined by a visible seam.

Despite all the technology, the GT750 was overshadowed by Kawasaki's two-stroke triples, which weren't water-cooled but were considerably quicker. Nevertheless, the Water Buffalo sold fairly well and continued until 1977, when it was replaced by a "conventional" four-cylinder four-stroke.

192

When introduced in 1971, Suzuki's "Water Buffalo" wasn't the typical two-stroke motorcycle. At 738 ccs, the engine was about 50-percent larger than any production two-stroke before it and water-cooled to boot—rare for any bike at the time. Furthermore, most two-strokes were light; but at 524 pounds, the GT750 was even heavier than Honda's 750 Four. Exhaust was routed through a "three-into-four" arrangement, with exhaust from the center cylinder being split between the two smaller mufflers. Note "figure 8" taillight lens.

1975 Triumph Trident

In an attempt to fend off the attack of Japanese exports to the lucrative U.S. market, Triumph and BSA released a pair of three-cylinder models. The Triumph T150 Trident and BSA Rocket 3 were introduced in the States during the summer of 1968.

Despite the fact that the two companies had joined forces in 1951 and the motorcycles themselves were similar in specification, the Trident and Rocket 3 differed in many respects. Styling was unique to each, and even the engines were slightly different: the Trident had vertically mounted cylinders, while those on the Rocket 3 were canted forward a bit.

While both were considered decent motorcycles that challenged the best in terms of performance, their strengths paled with the introduction of Honda's 750 Four a few months later. Both British bikes received minor updates in subsequent years, but the Rocket 3 dropped out of the picture in 1973 (along with BSA itself), while the Trident got an overhaul.

The revised Trident, called the T160, carried several new features. The most obvious change was the adoption of inclined cylinders that allowed for a slightly lower profile. The engine also was fitted with more durable internal hardware and gained an electric starter. To appeal to American tastes (and laws), the shift lever was moved to the left side of the bike. A 10-inch disc brake finally appeared up front to replace the antiquated drum.

Unfortunately for Triumph, the superbike ante had been raised by the likes of Kawasaki's new Z-1, and though certainly improved, the Trident just didn't measure up. Furthermore, the displacement of its Bonneville twin-cylinder sibling had been increased to the same 750 ccs in 1973, and few buyers could justify the Trident's higher price. As a result, Triumph's triple faded from the scene after 1976, though the name was revived in 1990 for a more modern, water-cooled, three-cylinder machine to be produced by a new Triumph corporation.

The second-generation Trident received some subtle changes, including an electric starter and cylinders that went from vertical to slightly inclined. It also got a left-side shifter and front disc brake. The center exhaust port was split, allowing the center pipe to join with each of the outer ones, and each pair then routed into its own muffler. The X-75, designed by Craig Vetter of fairing fame, was a styling exercise based on the Trident. It featured sleek, cafe-racer bodywork and a prominent three-muffler exhaust system. A fair number were sold through Triumph dealers, and are very valuable today.

X-75

1976 Hercules W2000

Looking back over the history of motorcycling, it's evident that a wide variety of powerplants have been used. From the very first steam-powered units to the multivalve electronic wonders of today, there was very little that wasn't attempted.

Hercules started building motorcycles in 1904, and for many years designed its own chassis but used proprietary engines. This policy continued until 1966, when the company was merged with DKW under Fichel & Sachs Company. Afterward, the Hercules name typically adorned mopeds. But something really new was on the horizon.

In an effort to combine efficiency and smooth power delivery, a rotary engine was slipped into a Hercules frame. Powered by a Sachs 292-cc, single-rotor Wankel, the W2000 was the first commercially built Wankel-powered motorcycle.

The prototype W2000 had its Wankel engine mated to a BMW gearbox with shaft drive, but production versions got a different transmission with six speeds and were chain-driven. While the Wankel was indeed a silky powerplant, it generated excess heat, and the W2000 was never sold in great numbers.

Another Wankel-powered motorcycle was made by Suzuki in the mid Seventies. Featuring a water-cooled 500-cc single-rotor Wankel, the RE-5 proved to be unreliable, and it too was quickly discontinued.

Suzuki RE-5

If the engine's appearance didn't give away the W2000's secret, the side-panel badge left no doubt. Sachs rotary carried a large fan up front, but it proved insufficient to keep the Wankel from overheating; note the rather modest cooling fins, no doubt a contributing factor in the problem. Suzuki released its rotary-powered RE-5 at about the same time as the W2000, but it featured a larger-displacement Wankel of about 500 ccs and was marketed as more of a sport-tourer.

1976 Moto Guzzi V1000 Convert

After boosting its V-twin from 700 ccs to 750 ccs and then 850 ccs, Moto Guzzi made the jump to a full liter. One of the first recipients of the bigger V-twin was a new model called the V1000 Convert.

"Convert" stood for converter—as in torque converter. Power was fed from the engine through a torque converter to a conventional clutch. Though the big Guzzi still used a transmission, it had only two speeds. The clutch had to be disengaged to manually shift between low and high gear, but thanks to the torque converter, the rider could come to a complete stop in either gear and then accelerate away without touching the clutch or the gearshift lever.

By this time, some of the company's products were focused on the sport-touring market, but the V1000 Convert was never considered as such. For one thing, it tipped the scales at nearly 600 pounds and was not well-suited to fast cornering. It also didn't accelerate with much verve, as the weight, gear ratios, and torque converter all contributed to lackluster performance. But as a pure touring machine, it had much to offer.

The two-speed transmission and torque converter conspired to dull acceleration, so the V1000 was more at home on long tours or in stop-and-go driving, where the driver needed to neither shift nor de-clutch when coming to a stop. With Moto Guzzi's unusual triple-disc braking system, the foot pedal applied the rear brake and one of the front discs, while the hand lever operated the other front disc. Speedometer is flanked by a bevy of warning lights—but no tachometer. Two-speed transmission carried a handy heel-and-toe shifter. Note "lunch box" side bags and taillight housing.

1976 Norton Commando

Norton's Commando series bowed in 1968 to great fanfare, but by the mid Seventies had grown long in the tooth. Originally offered with a 750-cc twin, it was decided that a power boost was in order to help stem the tide of the Japanese onslaught.

The engine itself was going on 30 years old, but it was a solid design, and Norton increased its displacement to 850 ccs in what would turn out to be its final incarnation. Along with the larger engine came a front disc brake, joined later by a rear disc. In addition, U.S.-spec left-side shift was adopted, the dual seat was now hinged for convenience, and the speedometer and tachometer found themselves joined by a warning-light console.

Despite these efforts, Norton found itself deeper and deeper in financial muck. Merged with AJS and Matchless back in the Sixties, Norton was folded in with BSA and Triumph in the Seventies. BSA dropped out after 1973, leaving Triumph

and Norton to soldier on alone. They didn't march very far.

Though Triumph struggled along on its own for a few years afterward, Norton ceased production in 1977. However, both marques made cameo appearances during the Eighties, Norton fielding a Wankel-powered model that was produced in small numbers.

By 1976, the Commando had adopted front and rear disc brakes, left-side shift, and an electric starter, features that made it more attractive to American riders. The speedometer and tachometer were joined by a quartet of warning lights. The venerable Norton overhead-valve twin was by now long out of date, but still provided strong performance to the relatively lightweight machine.

1976 Triumph Bonneville

Throughout its long history, Triumph had faced numerous periods of financial strife. But the influx of high-performance, low-cost Japanese rivals in the Seventies prompted its biggest challenge to date.

Due to the cash-strapped position of the company, changes to the T140V Bonneville for 1976 were few, the most notable being that the drum brake on the rear wheel was finally replaced with a modern disc. The previous year, the gear-shift lever was moved to the left side to conform to U.S. government mandate. Rubber fork gaitors were not usually seen on European-spec Bonnevilles, but were standard equipment on T140s bound for the United States. Color choices were restricted to blue or red with white accent panels.

As a historical landmark, the 1976 Bonnevilles were the first to be built under the new Meriden financial cooperative. The cooperative folded in 1983, but the Bonneville stumbled on into 1988, the final years of production being handled by Les Harris under license from Triumph.

Bonneville's overhead-valve twin, which had been around since the mid Sixties, had received a boost from 650 ccs to 750 in 1973, and in '75 got a left-side shifter. As in earlier Bonnevilles, the tachometer displayed no redline.

1977 Ducati 900SS

Ducati's domination on the racetracks across Europe has led to the development of some exceptional road-going machines. With the debut of the 750SS and its desmodromic valvetrain in 1974, Ducati reached a new plateau of performance. Easily able to reach velocities in excess of 120 mph in a single bound, the 750SS reintroduced the world to Italian superbikes.

In 1976, a more powerful version of the SS appeared. Based on the non-desmodromic 860GT introduced in late 1973, the new 900SS added desmodromics to the larger engine, pushing the performance envelope even further.

With a top speed of over 140 mph, the 900SS was as fast as anything the Japanese had to offer. The carefully sculpted steel fuel tank was surrounded by a bullet-shaped half fairing, and the solo saddle was backed by an aerodynamic tailpiece. Together, these elements created a true racing image for the 900SS, which was only strengthened when Mike Hailwood rode a race-prepped version to victory at the Isle of Man TT.

The 900SS, introduced in 1976, carried an 860-cc V-twin fitted with Ducati's famous desmodromic valvetrain, which closed the valves mechanically rather than with springs; this virtually eliminated high-rpm valve float. As a result, the tachometer shows an 8000-rpm redline—quite high for a large-displacement twin. Note that the cooling fins on the forward cylinder run in a different direction than those on the rear cylinder due to the direction of air flow. Dual ventilated front disc brakes provided needed reassurance given the bike's high-speed potential.

1977 Harley-Davidson XLCR

In an attempt to capitalize on the café-racing trend that was sweeping the country in the mid Seventies, Harley-Davidson ventured back into the world of customs to bring out the XLCR. It applied a small "bikini" fairing, skimpy front fender, angular fuel tank, solo seat with fiberglass tail section, triple disc brakes, and special "siamesed" two-into-two exhaust headers to a standard 1000-cc Sportster, and then cloaked the whole affair in black.

The problem was that although the XLCR was claimed to be "the most powerful production cycle Harley-Davidson has ever built," that wasn't saying much; Japanese competitors were quite a bit quicker and cheaper to boot. Furthermore, the typical Harley buyer seemed to take little interest in joining the road-racing crowd, so sales never took off, and what was in fact a very interesting motorcycle (and quite soon, a very collectible motorcycle) faded away after only two years.

A sinister-looking road racer to be sure, the XLCR was nonetheless humbled by cheaper Japanese machines of the day; "siamesed" exhaust headers helped extract maximum power from the 1000-cc V-twin, but that just wasn't enough. Note that the shift lever was reversed on its shaft to make it accessible to the rear-set footpegs. An ad for the XLCR credits "Willie G." Davidson—grandson of one of the founders and designer of the famed Super Glide of 1971—with the concept.

1977 MV Agusta 750S America

MV Agusta's glorious racing background gave rise to numerous street bikes over the years, one of the last being the 750S America. Introduced in 1975, it featured blockier styling and a larger engine than previous 750s.

The 790-cc double-overhead-cam four-cylinder engine in the 750S America had its roots in a 500-cc racing powerplant. When shipped from the factory, the stock exhaust system was an odd combination of chrome downtubes with megaphones finished in black crinkle paint. The exhaust seen here is a Magni design and looks more the part. Arturo Magni was the man responsible for nearly all of MV's racing success. When his designs were put into the hands of riders like Mike Hailwood, the competition had little hope of winning.

The sleek half-fairing is another popular Magni accessory and was also available in a full Gran Prix configuration. Weighing 507 pounds without fluids,

the 750S is no lightweight, but its handling at speed belies the mass. The suede-covered racing saddle does its best to keep the pilot in place during the kind of spirited cornering maneuvers the 750S is so adept at performing.

Like previous MVs, the 750S America was expensive, yet the company continued to lose money. A change of ownership in 1977 did little to help matters, and production ceased during 1980.

But the revered MV Agusta name did not die. Nearly 20 years later it was revived by Cagiva, another Italian motorcycle manufacturer, to be used on an ultra-sport model called the F4. Though an initial run of a couple hundred units sold out quickly at about $40,000 apiece, regular production versions, called F4S, are to have less exotic materials and sell for about half that amount. In both performance and price, these new machines appear to be true spiritual successors to the MVs of old.

Like previous MV engines, cases on the 750S America look flat and characterless. Big power is produced within, however, with the redline set at 8500 rpm. Looking down at the tank, riders are reminded of MV's 37 Manufacturers World Championships. Suede saddle helped keep the pilot in place. Magni exhaust was not standard, though many bikes were later fitted with it.

1978 Harley-Davidson FXS

Harley-Davidson's first "factory custom" was released in 1971, setting the stage for many more to follow. Called the FX Super Glide, it combined the frame and engine from the big FL-series twins with the front forks and other trim pieces from the XL Sportster—hence the FX designation.

In the middle of 1977, Harley rolled out the FXS Low Rider. Like the Super Glide, it was based on the big FL series frame with a 74-cubic-inch V-twin. With a seat height of only 27 inches, the FXS fit almost any rider. In looks and concept, it contrasted sharply with Harley's other new entry for 1977, the XLCR. While the Sportster-based XLCR was square and sporty, the FXS had a low, muscular flow to its profile.

In 1978, the Low Rider's first full year of production, it outsold all other models in Harley's line, accounting for nearly 20 percent of total sales. The FXS was initially sold only in metallic gray with orange script, but black and white were offered late in the model year.

On the FXS, fuel is stored in the split "Fat Bob" tanks, which give the bike a substantial look. The 1978 version still carried both kick and electric starters, and the final drive was handled with a multi-row chain.

Though it was the first full year for the Low-Rider, 1978 turned out to be the last year for the venerable 74-cubic-inch V-twin, as Harley increased the displacement to 80 cubic inches for 1979.

Continuing the formula used for the original Super Glide of 1971, the first Low Rider featured the frame and engine from the FL-series "Big Twins" supported by the front end of the smaller XL Sportster models. Big 74-cubic-inch V-twin exhaled through a two-into-one header. A matte-black finish was used on the instrument panel and upper tank trim.

1978 Kawasaki Z1-R and Z1-R TC

Kawasaki's 900-cc four-cylinder Z-1 of 1973 set new standards for motorcycle performance, yet company officials were soon discussing the idea of building a "special" version of the successful model. Since the café-racer look was in vogue at the time, the decision was made to create their own variation.

Using existing blueprints for the soon-to-be-released KZ1000, the Z1-R was intended to be little more than a styling exercise. The fuel tank was drawn up using flat, angular lines that were mimicked by the triangular side panels and sharply creased front fender. The fiberglass fairing followed suit, and all the bodywork was sprayed with specially blended Ice Blue metallic paint that was used only on the Z1-R.

The frame was the same as the original Z-1 of 1973, but several improvements were made to complement the exclusive nature of the R model. Its 1015-cc engine exhausted through the industry's first factory-installed four-into-one header system, while triple disc brakes with drilled rotors redefined stopping power.

Extensive use of fiberglass for the body components helped reduce weight, and combined with the free-breathing nature of the engine, allowed the Z1-R to become the first stock street bike to record sub-12-second runs in the standing-start quarter-mile. Styling exercise indeed.

For those still not satisfied, however, there was an aftermarket turbocharger kit for the bike. Often dealer installed, an example so equipped was known as a Z1-R TC. The turbo raised power to a phenomenal level for the time, and likely influenced factory-built turbocharged models from other Japanese companies, and eventually Kawasaki itself.

A bikini fairing, squared-off lines, and special Ice Blue paint identified a Z1-R. An aftermarket turbo kit turned it into a Z1-R TC, probably the quickest bike of its day. Note the exhaust plumbing required to route gases to the TC's turbo. A boost gauge added to the stock instruments helped keep tabs on internal pressures.

1978 Moto Guzzi LeMans

When Moto Guzzi introduced its first V-twin in the mid Sixties, it displaced 700 ccs and was mounted in a shaft-drive model called the V7. The engine soon grew to 750 ccs, and a performance-oriented model called the Sport followed.

Further enlargements to the V-twin in the mid Seventies in- creased displacement to 850 ccs, and then to a full liter. Most were mounted in touring motorcycles, but in order to capture the attention of the enthusiast market, Moto Guzzi introduced the LeMans Mk I in 1976.

Like other Moto Guzzis of the period, the LeMans was built on a tubular frame, a section of which could be unbolted to allow for easy removal of the engine. It also had a linked braking system where the foot pedal controlled not only the rear disc, but also one of the twin front discs; the other was activated by the conventional hand-brake lever. Unique to the LeMans was a bikini fairing, clip-on handlebars, and distinct badging and trim.

Though not in the same performance league as Japanese superbikes, the LeMans offered a unique blend of V-twin torque and Italian style, and would remain in production for some time to come. Dual ventilated front disc brakes were backed up by a single ventilated disc in the rear.

1980 Honda CX500

When Honda introduced the CX500 in 1978, it seemed as though the company had intentionally set out to create the weirdest bike it could envision. Virtually every aspect broke long-established molds.

First, the powertrain: While V-twins were nothing unusual and Moto Guzzi had been mounting them "crosswise" in the frame with shaft drive for many years, this Honda was decidedly different. Not only was the 500-cc engine water cooled, but it had four valves per cylinder that were operated by pushrods rather than more conventional overhead cams.

Furthermore, styling was questionable at best. Upright forks and a short engine contributed to a stubby wheelbase on a bike that was itself rather tall. The CX500 was one of the first recipients of Honda's new Comstar "mag" wheels, which measured 19 inches in front but only 16 in back, and the look took awhile to get used to. But all of that paled next to the sheet-metal. The fuel tank tapered toward the front, and a huge half-moon taillight jutted out from a short fairing behind the radically stepped seat. The end result was an odd mix of standard, sport, and cruiser features.

Strangely enough, the CX500 met with a fair degree of success. It proved to be reliable and economical, and despite rather high prices for a 500, was one of the least-expensive shaft-drive bikes around. The rather awkward-looking initial versions proved popular with police departments and commuters, while later Custom variants were easier on the eyes, and a touring-oriented Silver Wing (sort of a baby Gold Wing) made for a nice lightweight road bike. And though performance was never a CX500 selling point, that was about to change....

CX500 Custom

Proving both economical and reliable, the shaft-drive CX500 became popular with police departments. The "crosswise" V-twin was water-cooled and sported four valves per cylinder—which, oddly, were pushrod operated. Odd-looking initial versions were soon joined by a Custom model that carried more focused styling.

1981 BMW R65

Buyers admiring BMW's long-standing reputation for building dependable machines found that it came at a price—a rather high price. So in 1979, BMW built the first R65 as an entry-level model for those who would otherwise be unable to afford the cost of admission.

Powered by a 650-cc version of BMW's traditional horizontally opposed twin, the R65 was really just a scaled-down edition of the company's larger 1000-cc model. As a result, what was lost in sheer power was replaced with manageability; weighing in at only 452 pounds with a full tank of fuel, the R65 was more nimble at slow speeds.

Although identical to the original R65 in appearance, the 1981 version boasted several improvements. All BMWs that year gained transistorized ignitions to replace the old points-and-condenser systems. Cast sleeves were discarded in favor of

Nikasil coating for the cylinders, and the intake and exhaust valves were enlarged to improve breathing. Oil pan capacity was also increased.

Despite all the improvements, the 1981 models carried a list price that was $235 less than the year before, allowing more hopeful BMW enthusiasts to walk into their local dealer and ride home on a new R65.

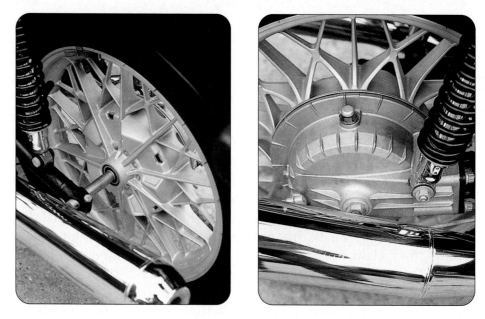

Despite its mission as a low-cost, entry-level model, the R65 carried traditional BMW virtues. Overhead-valve 650-cc flat twin was bred for smoothness and reliability rather than speed, but offered good low-rpm pulling power. Dual ventilated disc brakes slowed the front wheel, while the rear drum was beautifully integrated into the cast rear wheel.

1981 Ducati Hailwood Replica

Mike Hailwood began his racing career at the tender age of 18. Initially riding for the MZ Gran Prix team, "Mike the Bike" would later make the move to Ducati. During his career, he would chalk up nine world championships and claim victory in over 70 Gran Prix events. It seemed only fitting that the replica built to commemorate his success would turn out to be Ducati's best-selling model in the early Eighties.

Cloaked in the familiar red, white, and green of the Italian flag, the replica looks every inch a race bike. The GP-style front fairing is a one-piece affair that was later divided into two sections to allow for simpler access to the hardware that lurks within.

The race-proven 860-cc V-twin, complete with desmodromic valvetrain, seems right at home in the traditional Ducati birdcage chassis. The flowing two-into-one exhaust exits on the left side of the bike, and does little to mask the raucous note put out by the engine.

The extremely short clip-on handlebars help fulfill the illusion of riding a true GP machine, but make parking a nightmare. Hidden beneath the fiberglass tail section is a spot reserved for a brave and durable riding partner since comfort is not a consideration on a race machine—or a replica.

Ducati's unique desmodromic valve actuation system is driven by a single overhead camshaft. Unlike most OHC engines, which use a chain to spin the cam, Ducati uses a shaft and bevel gears; this example carries a window through which the motion can be viewed. Fuel tank is fitted with a racing-inspired gas cap and vent/overflow tube. Tachometer indicates a redline of 8000 rpm—quite high for a large-displacement twin.

1981 Harley-Davidson Heritage Edition

Harley-Davidson celebrated its 75th Anniversary in 1978, and one of the product highlights of that year was the return of an 80-cubic-inch V-twin, absent from the line since World War II. Soon afterward, the "retro" look came into vogue at Harley-Davidson, a styling trend that continues to this day. One of the first products to combine these two features was the 1981 Heritage Edition.

Carrying a two-place saddle, headlight nacelle, green and orange paint, and other features seen on classic Harleys of yesteryear (but equipped with modern suspension and brakes), only 784 Heritage Editions were built for 1981, and the model did not return in '82. With its time-honored styling and low production numbers, the Heritage itself has now become a coveted classic.

But perhaps overshadowing any of Harley-Davidson's product offerings in 1981 was a much larger event that took place in June of that year. After more than a decade under the AMF banner, a group of Harley-Davidson employees arranged financing and bought back the company. While production and profits both increased under AMF, quality didn't. After the buyout, employees and enthusiasts alike took a new pride in Harley-Davidson.

For those who might wonder what to call the green and orange dresser, the front fender spelled it out for them. A Heritage Edition emblem also graced the engine's primary cover. By this time, Harley had moved the choke knob to a more convenient location on the instrument panel, where the owner's name could be engraved on a special Heritage Edition plaque. A mixture of old and new graced the fuel tank; old-style lettering, but with the AMF logo. The latter would be the first thing to go after employees bought Harley-Davidson back from AMF in the summer of '81.

1981 Honda CBX

Honda's mighty CBX was introduced in 1978 amidst a chorus of technical fanfare. While it was not the first motorcycle to be powered by a six-cylinder engine, it was the latest and arguably the most advanced entry into the hotly contested superbike battle being fought by the Japanese manufacturers.

Despite its impressive brawn and intimidating six-pipe exhaust system, the CBX never really caught on with the street-racing crowd. Some competitors were cheaper, lighter, and (most importantly) quicker, so the big

Honda was often dismissed as being more show than go.

Failing to capture its intended audience, Honda switched gears and headed the CBX into the sport-touring category. Adding a sleek fairing and custom-fitted saddle bags transformed the six-cylinder machine into an impressive road bike, its buttery-smooth engine affording effortless cruising at better than 100 miles per hour.

Suspension also played a major role in the big bike's comfort. Fitted with air-adjustable shocks at both ends, the CBX's suspension could easily be tuned to the

rider's liking. And helping to haul its 680-pound heft down from triple-digit speeds were dual stainless-alloy ventilated front rotors—a first for the motorcycle industry.

Yet, in spite of its touring credentials, the CBX "dresser" did not fare much better than its stripped-down predecessor, and production of Honda's six-cylinder wonder ceased at the end of the 1982 model year. But with its sparkling waterfall of exhaust pipes, it's unlikely the CBX in either guise will ever be written off by collectors as just another Japanese motorcycle.

CBX's signature was its waterfall of gleaming exhaust pipes. Rear saddlebags could be detached and carried like a briefcase. Small "ducktail" spoiler on the front fender between the fork tubes directed air over the oil cooler and 24-valve heads. Due to government regulations in force at the time, the speedometer only registered to 85 mph—which the CBX could easily exceed in third gear. An early ad for the machine states that "The Honda CBX is here...to stay." Yes, but only for five years.

1981 Yamaha 1100 Midnight Special

Yamaha was one of the first Japanese manufacturers to embrace "cruiser" styling in the late 1970s, beginning with the vertical-twin 650 Special and culminating in its V-twin Viragos. The success of those models quickly spawned copycats (and to be fair, the Virago itself attempted to mimic offerings from Harley-Davidson), some of which grew out of Yamaha's own product line.

One such example was the 1100 Midnight Special, one of several models adorned with a unique black-and-gold color scheme. Based on the company's big XS1100 sport-tourer introduced in the late '70s, the 1100 Midnight Special differed from most of its ilk in having a traditional Japanese inline four-cylinder engine rather than the trendy V-twin. It also featured shaft drive, likewise carried over from the XS.

While an extended fork, teardrop tank, and stepped saddle made it clear this was a cruiser, the double-overhead-cam four-cylinder engine gave it powerful performance unmatched by contemporary V-twins. Parts that would normally be chromed were covered in "black chrome," such as the exhaust pipes and handlebars, or "gold chrome," as were the air-cleaner cover and rear grab rail.

But while the cruiser trend continues to this day, Yamaha's various Midnight Specials had a fairly short run. And in the case of the 1100, it was also a small run. With just 250 built for 1980 and another 250 in '81, they are rare commodities today.

Gold trim dressed the wheels and all three disc brakes, along with the differential for the shaft drive. "Black chrome" covered the exhaust pipes, while "gold chrome" graced the air-cleaner cover.

1982 Harley-Davidson FXB Sturgis

For over half a century, the annual trek to the Black Hills of South Dakota has become a ritual for many motorcycle enthusiasts. One week each summer, the town of Sturgis teems with motorcyclists from around the country, and in 1982, Harley-Davidson decided to commemorate the event with the release of the FXB Sturgis.

As denoted by the "FX" prefix in the nomenclature, the FXB is based on the Low Rider chassis and engine. The big difference is the "B" suffix, which in this instance stands for belts; both the primary and final drives are fitted with toothed belts in lieu of the typical chains. Although more difficult to repair, the dual belt system provides clean, quiet, and mostly trouble-free operation. Starting of the FXB's 80-cubic-inch "Shovelhead" V-twin can be accomplished by either pushing a button or kicking a lever. An electronic ignition alleviated some earlier problems, making the big twin easier to fire up.

The Sturgis is clothed in black with just enough chrome and color to make things interesting. A two-inch extension of the front forks gives it a "chopper" look. The fuel tank is topped with a speedometer, tachometer, and matching filler caps.

Like virtually all of Harley's early customs, the Sturgis is now a collector's piece. Unlike some of the others, however, it was a hit right from the start.

Unique to the Sturgis in '82 was dual belt drive, with toothed belts substituting for chains in both the primary (engine to transmission) and final drive (transmission to rear wheel). Likewise, black trim took the place of brightwork on many components such as the tank-mounted instrument cluster, "ham can" air cleaner, and headlight cover.

1982 Honda MB-5

In 1980, the concurrent trends toward scooters and sportbikes collided in Honda's MB-5. Though seemingly odd bedfellows, the little commuter bike certainly had its admirers.

Sporty looks aside, the MB-5 was no scorcher, its 50-cc two-stroke single being aimed more at economy than speed. But several "big bike" features could be found, including speedometer and tachometer (the latter redlined at a dizzying 10,500 rpm), front disc brake, and Honda's Comstar wheels. A two-place saddle was fitted, though surely the little engine would be taxed carrying a pair of passengers.

Unique and endearing as it was, the MB-5 was short-lived in the U.S. Other manufacturers didn't jump on the idea, and Honda abandoned the MB-5 after just a few years.

Front disc brake seemed like overkill on a bike with such modest speed potential, but probably helped inspire confidence in new riders.

Sporty as it looked, the MB-5's little 50-cc two-stroke didn't produce much power, even at its 10,500-rpm redline. Comstar wheels could be found on Honda's big bikes.

1982 Kawasaki KZ1000R

During the 1970s, Japanese manufacturers jumped on the superbike craze, turning out some impressive machines for the consumer. At about the same time, a fellow named Eddie Lawson was turning out some impressive lap times on his 250-cc Kawaski race bike. With the creation of the competition Superbike class, Mr. Lawson switched to larger street-based machines, often putting them in the winner's circle.

To commemorate these feats, Kawasaki released the KZ1000R, otherwise known as the Eddie Lawson Replica, or ELR for short. Based on the standard KZ1000, it sported the same 1015-cc double-overhead-cam inline four, but with a special four-into-one Kerker exhaust header as standard equipment (Kerker enjoying second billing on the fuel tank). Painted in "Kawasaki racing green," the ELR was also fitted with a small bikini fairing that probably did little to protect the rider, but added a competition look—as did the blacked-out engine.

Stiffer front suspension and special "piggyback" reservoir rear shocks aided roadholding, while triple disc brakes brought the whole affair to a halt.

Relatively few KZ1000Rs were built, making them rare when new and even more rare today. But Kawasaki has recently revived the spirit of the KZ1000R by

releasing an updated replica (making it a replica of a replica) called the ZRX1100.

Widely known as the Eddie Lawson Replica, the KZ1000R wore the company's distinctive green racing colors. Kawasaki's 1015-cc double-overhead-cam four revved happily to 9000 rpm, and proved to be a strong and durable engine—on both street and track. Suspension improvements included gold-painted "piggyback" reservoir rear shocks. A decal on the tank reminded riders of Kawasaki's racing victories.

1983 Honda CX650T

The sportbike battle had been raging for a good ten years when Honda introduced a new and innovative competitor: the CX500 Turbo. Not only was it the world's first turbocharged production bike, it also featured fuel injection and the most radical fairing yet seen on a motorcycle.

The Turbo's powerplant was based on the water-cooled V-twin with four pushrod-operated overhead valves per cylinder used in the shaft-drive CX500 introduced a few years earlier—itself a groundbreaking design. The base engine also was used in the Silver Wing, a touring machine aimed at being the Gold Wing's little brother, and a Custom model with "chopper" styling.

In 1983, both versions of the V-twin were bumped to 650 ccs. For the new CX650 Turbo, that meant a boost from 77 to 97 horsepower, making it one of the more powerful motorcycles available that year. Otherwise, it was mostly a carryover from the CX500 Turbo, although the color scheme was changed from pearlescent eggshell with red and black accents to the pearlescent white with red and blue trim as shown on our featured bike.

With their complex fuel injection systems and related sensors and actuators, the CX Turbos carried high prices and were a nightmare for shade-tree mechanics. And while spiraling insurance rates were affecting all performance bikes, many insurers looked unfavorably at turbocharged models in particular, assessing them with exorbitant premiums. So although the whistle of the turbo and resulting kick of acceleration boiled the adrenaline of those who rode one, the CX650 Turbo—along with the imitators that soon followed—sadly suffered a premature extinction.

The CX's V-twin was unusual in that each of the head's four valves were operated by pushrods rather than over-head cams. Mounted "side-ways" in the frame *à la* Moto Guzzi, the rather pedestrian engine grew significantly stronger with the addition of electronic fuel injection and a turbocharger. More sedate versions of the CX sold far better than the complicated and expensive Turbo.

1983 Suzuki Katana 1100

Suzuki was the last of the Japanese manufacturers to add road-going four-strokes to its line, that event finally coming with the introduction of the four-cylinder GS750 in 1976. Fitted with dual overhead cams (but only two valves per cylinder), it was slightly quicker than the venerable Honda 750, but that Honda was no longer the performance target to shoot for.

Inevitably, larger Suzukis followed, and not far behind. A GS1000 was introduced the next year, and made a big splash as being among the most powerful and best-handling Japanese fours available. But no bike stayed at the top for long during this period, and competitors quickly overshadowed it.

At a time when superbikes were beginning to take on fairings and other sporting touches, Suzuki was again falling behind the leaders. In an attempt to make up ground, the company brought out the Katana.

Powered by a new generation of dual-overhead-cam four-valve-per-cylinder engines, the Katanas arrived in 1982 in 750- and 1000-cc sizes, the latter growing to 1100 ccs for '83. Compared with Suzuki's "standard" motorcycles—and even with other manufacturer's sport models—the Katanas looked to be from outer space. An oddly sculptured wedge-shaped fairing sat above a half-moon front fender and ahead of an angled fuel tank. Vertical side covers contained multiple slats and a circular fuel valve. Seats were divided; one color on the front half, another color at the rear. It was decidedly different and certainly stood out, but the look prompted mixed reviews.

Though the name would carry on, the controversial first-generation Katanas would not. Subsequent Suzukis—even those that wore the Katana name—would more closely follow the status quo.

The Katana's bizarre styling set new standards for strangeness, from its half-moon front fender to its dual-tone seat. But it was hardly "all show and no go," as the 1100-cc four featured double overhead cams and four valves per cylinder. Handling was aided by a stiffer suspension with antidive forks.

1983 Yamaha XJ 650 Seca Turbo

Hot on the heels of Honda's CX Turbos came Yamaha's entry. Based on the company's four-cylinder 650 Seca, it surpassed the CXs in personality, if not performance.

Like Honda's models, it set new standards for aerodynamics, at least in appearance. The Seca wore a full fairing with deep spoiler under the engine to scoop up cooling air. Fuel tank and side panels flowed together into a tail section that surrounded the seat. If anything, it looked even more futuristic than the cutting-edge CX Turbo.

Power came from a pressurized double-overhead-cam 650 four cylinder as found in the standard Seca. Unlike some turbos, the Seca inhaled through four separate carburetors, exhaling through only one of its twin mufflers; the other exhausted overboost from the turbo.

Interesting as it was, the Seca Turbo failed to provide the "big bike" power it promised, and didn't last long in the marketplace. It faded away after just a couple of years, as did other turbo bikes before and since.

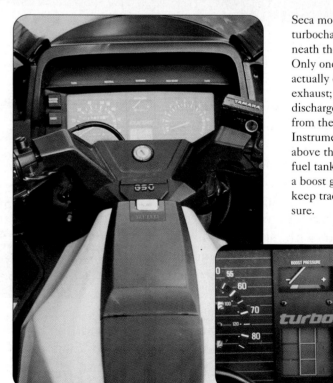

Seca mounted its turbocharger underneath the engine. Only one muffler actually carried exhaust; the other discharged overboost from the turbo. Instrument panel above the angled fuel tank contained a boost gauge to keep track of pressure.

1984 Harley-Davidson XR-1000 Sportster

Harley's XR-750 racing bike enjoyed such success on the nation's flat tracks that a street version was introduced in 1983 to capitalize on the notoriety. Though based on the stripped-down XLX Sportster, the XR-1000 was fitted with special cylinder heads similar to those found on the racing version. These had intake ports entering the rear of both cylinders fed by dual carburetors on the right-hand side, and front-exiting exhaust ports emptying into high-mounted dual mufflers that exited on the left. By contrast, all other Sportsters had a single carb (also on the right)

that fed to centrally mounted intake ports, with exhaust exiting on the right from outboard ports.

The modifications resulted in an output of nearly 70 horsepower, a figure only dreamed of by other Sportsters, and gave the XR-1000 acceleration unequaled by any other street motorcycle Harley had ever built.

Unfortunately, the race-bred hardware that made the XR-1000 quite fast also made it quite expensive. At nearly $2000 more than the XLX, not enough riders appreciated the difference, and the XR would fade into the sunset after the 1984 model run.

XR-750

It was all in the heads: The XR's twin carbs on the right fed into the back of both cylinders, while exhaust exited on the left from the front of the cylinders—entirely different from the standard Sportsters. The design originated on the XR-750 dirt-track race bike campaigned with great success throughout the Seventies and Eighties.

241

1984 Honda Nighthawk 700S

Based on the shaft-drive 650 Nighthawk introduced in 1983, the 700S was a sportier version brought out the following year. Due to tariffs then being levied against motorcycles over 700 ccs, the S replaced a 750 in Honda's line. But whereas the Nighthawk 650 and older chain-drive 750 were styled like "standard" motorcycles, the 700S sported angular lines capped by a bikini fairing and smaller 16-inch front wheel—then becoming the rage for sportbikes. The 700S came only in black, with either blue or red accent panels.

Power came from a slightly larger version of the 650's double-overhead-cam four—which featured hydraulic lifters that virtually eliminated valve adjustments—with a special four-into-one exhaust header finished in black chrome. The engine itself was enameled mostly in black, as were the lower fork legs, handlebars, and rear grab rail, pieces that were normally chromed.

Since full-tilt sportbikes of the era were gravitating toward a more radical look with full fairings and crouched seating positions, the 700S filled the gap between sport and standard motorcycles. Though a good compromise and a capable performer, the sharp-looking 700S lasted only a couple of years in the marketplace.

Unlike true sport-bikes, the 700S was fitted with low-maintenance shaft drive and hydraulic valve lifters; the latter would normally have limited engine speed, but an innovative new design from Honda allowed a lofty 10,600-rpm rev limit.

1985 Yamaha RZ 500

In the early 1980s, the marketing department at Yamaha sensed the need for an all-out performance machine. It had to be light in weight, look and behave like a Gran Prix bike, and be within budgetary guidelines. After several years of development, the RZ 500 shot out the Yamaha factory doors.

In a brash deviation from the norm, the RZ was powered by a 499-cc "square" four-cylinder two-stroke with twin cranks and liquid cooling. Somewhat more conventional was a chassis formed from square-section aluminum-alloy tubing. This choice of material allowed for superb stiffness matched with light weight.

The RZ's extraordinary performance and handling were actually seen as detriments to the average

rider, and sales of Yamaha's little pocket rocket were poor. Placed in the proper hands, it was a potent weapon on the track, but unfortunately a handful around town. Furthermore, the two-stroke powerplant excluded the RZ 500 from the list of machines available for sale in the United States, though several examples managed to find their way in anyhow.

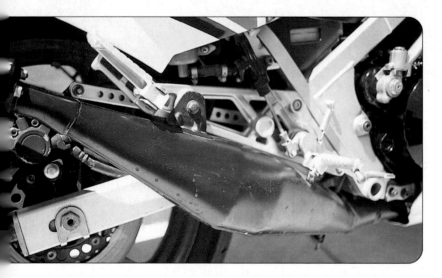

Wild twin-crank four-cylinder two-stroke was tame at low revs, but exploded to life as it neared its 10,000-rpm redline. A six-speed gearbox allowed the rider to keep the peaky two-stroke within its narrow power range. Exhaust flowed through four pipes; two in the normal position, two more jutting from either side of the taillight. Bulbous expansion chambers helped produce more power. Adjustable antidive mechanism on the forks was triggered by application of the front brakes.

1985 Yamaha V-Max

When introduced in 1985, the V-Max instantly became the undisputed King of Quick. Neither sportbike nor cruiser, the V-Max was simply a dragster for the street.

Power—and a prodigious amount it was—came from a 1200-cc V-four with four valves per cylinder. The engine was based on a powerplant from the company's Venture touring bike but with numerous modifications, among them a variable intake system that opened an extra set of butterflies as rpms increased, allowing great low-end torque along with 145 peak horsepower. Oddly, final drive was by shaft, which undoubtedly absorbed more power than would a chain, but the V-Max didn't seem to mind.

Fast the V-Max was; subtle it wasn't. What looked like a sliver of a fuel tank was actually just a cover for the electronics, as the tank itself was under the seat. Huge aluminum scoops beneath the tank looked like ram-air ducts, but actually hid the horns.

A lone speedometer sat atop the handlebars, with a tachometer, water temperature gauge, and warning lights situated in a "tank"-mounted instrument panel. A stepped saddle helped keep the rider in place during throttle applications, and a duck-tail rear fender was there to...well...just look racy.

Though discontinued after a couple of years, the V-Max made a comeback in the late Eighties. But it was a while longer before any motorcycle managed to top its straight-line performance.

The mighty V-Max owed its legacy to a 1200-cc four-valve V-four with variable intake runners and 145 horsepower. Nothing else of the day even came close. What appeared to be massive air scoops were really just covers for the horns, but they sure looked mean.

The speedometer was perched above the handlebars, while the tach, water-temperature gauge, and host of warning lights sat in a separate instrument panel. The "fuel tank" wasn't a tank at all, but a cover for the electronic components; fuel was stored in a tank beneath the seat.

1986 Ducati 750 F1 Montjuich

Ducati entered the motorcycle market after World War II with small-displacement, single-cylinder machines. Designer Fabio Taglioni arrived in the mid Fifties, adding a shaft-driven overhead cam and desmodromic valve actuation to Ducati's racing engines. By 1971, both these features were offered on some of the company's road-going models, and those single-cylinder Ducatis were potent machines.

Venturing into the sportbike market in 1971, Ducati introduced a 750-cc V-twin with the traditional shaft-driven cams and desmodromic valve gear. It was followed by larger-displacement versions that met with great success, and quickly took over Ducati's line.

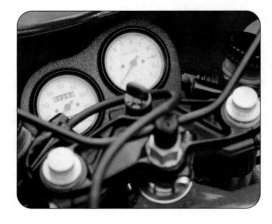

But there was a time when it appeared as though the Italian company, with its famous "desmo" powerplants, was on its last legs. Luckily for sportbike enthusiasts, Cagiva entered the picture and rescued the Ducati name from the brink of disaster.

To develop the Montjuich, which was named for the famous Montjuich Park Gran Prix circuit in Barcelona, Spain, Cagiva management lured Fabio Taglioni out of retirement to breath new life into the tired 90-degree V-twin. Having done so, Ducati assembled the rest of the motorcycle—sparing no expense—for racing homologation. Only 200 of the 750-cc bikes were built, a mere ten finding their way to the United States.

The Montjuich was a serious racing bike, which meant no passengers, no air filters, and no turn signals. Massive Brembo floating ventilated disc brakes were found front and rear, and dry weight was a mere 367 pounds.

1986 Suzuki GSXR750

As the sportbike battle grew ever more intense, the machines themselves grew closer and closer to street-legal racers. Few bikes illustrate that point better than the GSXR750.

Introduced for 1985, this latest entry from Suzuki was intended to reflect the technology learned from winning the World Endurance Championship in 1983 with a works GSXR. Differences between the two were minimal.

The GSXR's four-cylinder engine represented the third step in a technological progression. The GS of the late Seventies was a four cylinder with two valves per cylinder, the GSX of the early Eighties had four valves per cylinder, and the GSXR added oil cooling for better heat dissipation. Horsepower of the 750-cc version rose from 83 on the GSX to 100 on the GSXR—quite a boost. But that wasn't the bike's only advantage.

Wrapped around the engine was a box-section alloy frame that weighed significantly less than the former tubular steel one while being stiffer to boot. A crouched, racerlike riding position and full fairing further mimicked the competition version.

In all, the GSXR750 represented a quantum leap forward for Suzuki, if not the entire industry. And better still was yet to come….

Trend-setting dual round headlamps were set into a full fairing, while at the rear, a tapered, squared-off tail section held a rectangular taillight. The plastic cover behind the driver's seat could be removed to unveil a skimpy passenger's perch. The GSXR's air/oil-cooled engine was completely hidden by the fairing, but its presence could be verified by the dominant tachometer—redlined at 11,000 rpm.

1986 Suzuki RG 500 Gamma

The RG 500 Gamma was built to defend Suzuki's honor against Yamaha's new RZ 500. Though both were technical marvels, they were answers to a question no one was asking.

Being extremely light and driven by a potent two-stroke powerplant, the Gamma is a loose cannon, with a high, narrow power band and a throttle that acts like a light switch. Around town, the RG is docile and handles well, but spinning the tach into the upper reaches brings a whole new meaning to the word "peaky." An experienced rider on the proper roads will find the Gamma capable of tremendous speeds, but a novice will seldom be able to tap the potential.

Construction of the Gamma centers around an all-aluminum, box-section chassis. The engine is a two-stroke "square four" with two crankshafts—identical in concept to that used in the RZ 500—providing the pilot with 90 horsepower. With a dry weight of 340 pounds, the Gamma was almost 50 pounds lighter than its competition from Yamaha.

In the end, both Suzuki and Yamaha had overestimated the demand for a street-legal race bike and sales figures languished. Although never imported directly into the United States, a handful of Gammas found their way in from across the Canadian border.

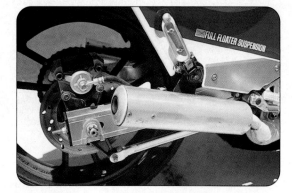

The Gamma's race-bike nature proved a bit high strung for practical street use, and that—combined with high prices—limited sales. Each of the four cylinders exhausted through its own muffler; two in the traditional location, two flanking the taillight; note the cooling vents for the latter. Six-spoke wheels featured very thin spokes. Gauges were prominently displayed, with the tachometer taking center stage. Namesake Greek letter "Gamma" is embossed in the upper frame rails.

1988 Harley-Davidson FLSTC

When introduced during the 1986 model year, the FLSTC was an instant hit. While it wasn't the first of Harley's retro-styled designs, it certainly set new standards for "Back to the Future" models.

Chief among its new retro features was Harley's Softail frame, introduced in 1984, which looked like hardtail frames of old yet incorporated modern rear-suspension technology. Other styling cues included beefy Hydra-Glide forks and skirted fenders, old-style tank lettering, "fishtail" muffler, frame-mounted tool box, front and rear fender lights, and studded seat and saddle bags.

In 1984, Harley-Davidson introduced the sixth generation of its Big Twin motor, the new arrival being called the Evolution V2. Replacing the "Shovelhead," which had been in use since 1966, the "Evo" (as it came to be called) remained an 80-cubic-inch overhead-valve design, but incorporated many refinements that made it smoother, more reliable, and more powerful. Only selected models got the Evo in '84—some continuing with the Shovel-head—but all had it the following year.

In deference to its retro theme, the FLSTC (which, deciphered, meant FL frame and forks, SofTail frame, Classic styling), was dubbed the Heritage Softail. The model has been so popular that a similar Heritage remains in the line to this day.

Dual spotlights had been common add-ons since the Fifties, and are no less useful today. Front-fender badge mimicked the lettering style used since the Hydra-Glide days of the late Forties, while tank decals dated to Harley's very early years.

1988 Harley-Davidson FXSTS Softail Springer

In what has become a common theme for Harley-Davidson, the FXSTS Softail Springer introduced in 1988 was designed with a combination of classic and modern styling elements. The new Springer front end, reminiscent of those used before Hydra-Glide hydraulic forks were introduced in 1949, employs a leading-link design activating compression and rebound springs, though they are now joined by a modern hydraulic shock. In back, the Softail suspension gives the look of a rigid frame, but instead pivots like a swingarm, extending a pair of coil-over shocks hidden beneath the chassis.

Back in the early Eighties, Harley had resurrected another idea from its past: belt drive. First appearing on a new Sturgis model, belts were used for both the primary drive (connecting the engine to the transmission) and secondary drive (transmission to rear wheel). Of course, they weren't leather belts as used in the early years, but rather toothed rubber belts with reinforcing strands. Lighter and quieter than chains, they required no lubrication. Compared to shaft-drive, they were cheaper and didn't invoke "pogoing" effects during throttle transitions. As a result, belt drive would prove to be a popular feature of many Harleys to come, including this one. Power for the Softail Springer came from the 80-cubic-inch overhead-valve "Evo" Big Twin that had replaced the "Shovelhead" of the same size a few years before.

The Softail Springer was one of three models selected during Harley-Davidson's 85th Anniversary year to wear special paint and badges commemorating the event. And this unique model remains a staple in the Harley-Davidson product line.

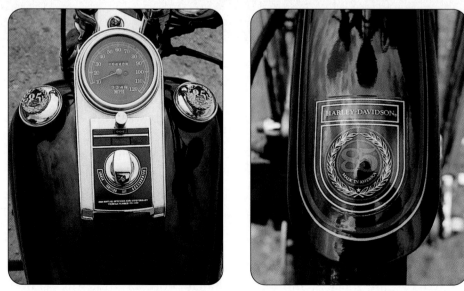

Harley's Softail rear suspension incorporates a triangulated swingarm that extends a pair of coil-over shocks mounted beneath the bike. Spring front fork is similar to those offered by Harley-Davidson prior to 1949, though it adds a shock absorber to improve control. Gas caps wear 85th Anniversary emblems, while similar decals grace the front fender and side of the fuel tank.

1988 Laverda SFC 1000

Laverda and the exoticar-maker Lamborghini share a common trait besides their Italian heritage: Both companies built farm implements before producing road-going machines.

Laverda's first motorcycle was a small, single-cylinder bike produced in the postwar era to test the waters of the market. It proved a raging success, and thus began the company's foray into motorcycle manufacturing.

At first, single-cylinder bikes were all Laverda produced. Then, in the late Sixties, the company ventured a vertical twin, considered quite a risk at the time. It wasn't until 1972 that triples were offered, and it is these for which Laverda is best known in the United States.

At first, the three-cylinder engines were fitted with single-plane (360-degree) crankshafts that produced uneven firing intervals and an ungainly exhaust note. Later, the crankshaft received staggered 120-degree throws, resulting in a smoother cadence and more power as well.

This SFC 1000 sport-touring model features a 981-cc triple that has amassed an enviable record in racing over the years. Marzocchi suspension at both ends combines a comfortable ride with capable handling, while a trio of disc brakes along with an antidive compensator fitted to the front forks ensure safe, controlled stops.

Because it was not intended for export, the SFC is a rare sight on U.S. roads. Yet, in many respects, it was better suited to American tastes than many of the exotic machines that found their way to these shores during the Eighties.

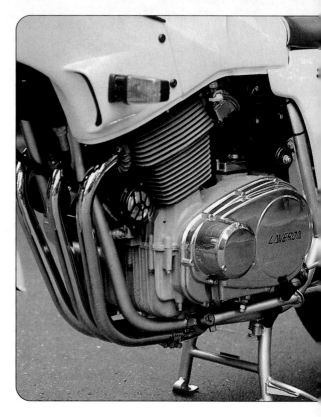

Aluminum gauge panel is dominated by a large tachometer redlined at 8000 rpm. Gold-painted frame, wheels, and suspension components added a classy touch to the SFC. Floating ventilated brake discs are gripped by Brembo calipers—about as close to a racing setup as you can get. With the shift to a new 120-degree crankshaft in the late Seventies, Laverda's triple gained both smoothness and power.

1989 Honda GB500 Tourist Trophy

By being named for the famed Tourist Trophy race held on England's Isle of Man, the GB500 made no secret of the fact that it sought to bring back the flavor of British twins that were, by the late Eighties, resigned to history. As a result, styling closely followed that of racing bikes from Norton's and Triumph's glory years on the track.

Shunning the fairings and 16-inch front wheels of contemporary Japanese sportbikes, the GB500 looked very much the part of a Sixties British racer with its standard-size spoke wheels, fork gaitors, clip-on handlebars, blocky fuel tank, and single seat with tail fairing. Even the 500-cc vertical twin with two-into-one header would strike a chord with fans of British machines, though the front disc brake gave a nod to modern technology.

Despite Honda's best efforts and intentions, sales never took off in the United States, and the GB500's life span was short.

1990 BMW K-1

Clad in futuristic plastic bodywork from stem to stern, the BMW K-1 looks more like a design study than a production model from the Black Forest. Based on the "Racer" design mockup done by BMW in 1984, the K-1 represents BMW's desire to appeal to a more youthful market.

The mechanicals found beneath the seven-piece skin are also a departure from BMW's standard fare. A 1000-cc, fuel-injected, sixteen-valve, water-cooled, inline four-cylinder engine propels the K-1 to a top speed of nearly 150 miles per hour. Final drive is handled by BMW's usual shaft, which is housed within the massive, bright yellow, single-sided swingarm. In front, four-piston calipers grip dual floating rotors. The rear wheel has its own disc brake, and the whole system is controlled by an ABS system to ensure safe stops even under less-than-ideal braking conditions.

Intended to compete in the sport-touring segment of the market, the K-1 is blessed with a large, comfortable seating area. The tail section of the bodywork can be removed to expose the passenger's pillion hiding below. Small storage compartments reside on each side of the tail piece, and each one has its own locking cover.

Through the 1980s, BMWs had been unique in design but conservative in execution. With bikes like the K-1 ringing in the '90s, BMW tipped its hand that future offerings would display a decidedly different side of its Teutonic nature.

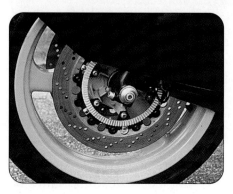

In a sleek departure from normal BMW practice, the K-1 featured a fully enclosed fairing—even the turn signals were faired in, both front and rear. "Toothed" trigger wheels for the antilock brake system ride inside the brake rotors; in front, the ABS sensor can be seen beneath the lower edge of the front fender. Single-sided swingarm incorporates a U-joint for the differential and a trailing arm to help position the wheel. Above the rear turn signals are small locking storage compartments. A driver's backrest is incorporated into the tail section, which can be removed to reveal a passenger's seat.

1990 Honda RC30

To the casual observer, the RC30 appears to be just another player in the current crop of fiberglass-bodied sport bikes. But to those in the know, it is nothing short of a thinly disguised racing machine.

First released to the Japanese market in the late 1980s, American enthusiasts had to wait until 1990 to get their hands on an RC30. Even then, a lofty price and limited availability made them a rare sight on public roads.

Though the 750-cc, double-overhead-cam V-4 will produce "just" 86 horsepower—not a class-leading figure by 1990—it contains race-inspired components such as titanium connecting rods that reduce reciprocating weight. Out front, the wheel and brake pads have quick-release mountings that smack of racing influence. Likewise the rear wheel, which carries a brake disc to the inside and a chain sprocket to the outside of a single-sided swingarm, and attaches with a single lug nut.

Yes, the RC30 may look like just another sports machine, but as we all know, looks can be deceiving.

The RC30's V-4 was fairly tame by sportbike standards of the day, yet the high-revving powerplant didn't redline until 12,500 rpm. At 475 pounds, the RC30 was no lightweight, but much of the componentry that contributed to that heft was strongly influenced by Honda's factory racers—and looked it. Huge floating disc brakes with twin-piston calipers nearly eclipsed the front wheel. Locking covers in the tail section hid a small storage area; seating was only for one.

1991 Harley-Davidson FXDB Sturgis

The first time Harley-Davidson produced a special model to commemorate the annual motorcycle rally in Sturgis, South Dakota, was in 1982. At that time, a Shovelhead V-twin sat between the frame rails; the 1991 version shown here was powered by the Evolution V-twin introduced in 1984—and it rested in a new Dynaglide chassis.

The 1991 Sturgis marked the 50th anniversary of the famed Black Hills rally. As with the first such model, the paint scheme centered around black with orange trim—Harley's corporate colors. Unlike most of the company's models, chrome was used sparingly, gracing only the forks, exhaust pipes, and miscellaneous trim bits.

Even the Sturgis's Evo V-twin was bathed in black, which, along with subtle orange accents, reflected the overall theme. Tank-mounted gauges followed standard Harley practice, but the housing was coated in wrinkle-finish black rather than the traditional chrome.

1992 Bimota Tesi

Bimota got its start in the early 1970s by wedding Honda or Kawasaki four-cylinder power with its own exotic chassis and bodywork, taking advantage of the fact that while the Japanese built state-of-the-art engines, the structures that contained them were somewhat underdeveloped. The marriage resulted in numerous racing victories, and frame kits were soon made available for the street.

The company's first complete motorcycle went on sale in 1977, that being the SB2 powered by a four-cylinder engine from Suzuki's GS750. Compared to the Japanese bike, the SB2 was lighter, faster, and handled better thanks to one of the industry's first monoshock rear suspensions and a lower center of gravity achieved by placing the fuel tank low in the frame. More potent models followed, powered by Kawasaki twin-cam fours of up to 1015 ccs.

Though Bimota had built up an enviable reputation by the early Eighties, the Japanese manufacturers had themselves begun to focus on handling, narrowing the advantages of the exclusive Italian make.

Still exorbitantly expensive, Bimotas lost much of their appeal—and much of their sales.

Salvation came in the form of the Ducati-powered DB1, an elemental sports machine that proved popular with buyers. It also established a link between the two Italian manufacturers that would continue for many years to come.

But perhaps the most exotic motorcycle to appear from the company known for innovation was the Tesi, released in the early Nineties. Joining the Ducati 904-cc V-twin and typical (for Bimota) full body cladding was a hub-center-steered front end that replaced the traditional forks. It used a swingarm similar to that found at the rear with the axle pivoting side-to-side within it.

According to the theory, steering and braking forces could be dealt with more easily, but it didn't turn out to be the great leap forward that Bimota had hoped. Furthermore, prices were high—even for a Bimota—and the complex mechanicals were not without their drawbacks. As a result, sales were slow and the technically advanced Tesi soon faded away.

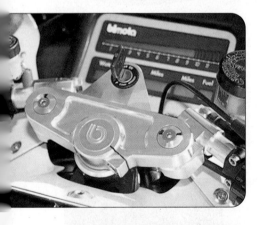

Space-age design extended to the cockpit, where digital instrumentation placed far more emphasis on engine rpm than vehicle speed. Though hub-center steering was not a new concept (other motorcycles had used it at least as far back as the Teens), it was novel in the Eighties, but ultimately, no more successful. The handlebars were connected to the lower red rod. When the handlebars were turned to the right, the rod pulled back on the black steering arm, which pivoted the hub to the right. The wheel rotated on a bearing mounted around the outside of the hub.

1992 Ducati 851 Desmoquattro

As the name implied, the 851 Desmoquattro, introduced in 1987, carried an 851-cc V-twin with Ducati's familiar desmodromic valve-train, but now with the blessing of four valves per cylinder. In addition, the 851 was water cooled and fed by electronic fuel injection. Power routed through a six-speed gearbox, and the combination helped racing versions rack up an enviable string of victories.

More importantly, perhaps, the 851 put Ducati back in the superbike game with a serious street contender, as previous versions were being over-shadowed by high-tech Japanese hardware. Though still down a bit on peak horsepower compared with some rivals, the 851 compensated with strong midrange punch, light weight afforded by exotic materials, and chassis dynamics second to none.

And the 851 was just a start. Its modern technology would form the basis for a string of even more potent street bikes, and is thus credited with ushering in a new era at Ducati.

Instrumentation was limited; the tachometer shows a lofty 10,000 rpm redline for the 851-cc desmodromic four-valve V-twin. Carbon-fiber mufflers and fenders helped keep weight down, and massive Brembo floating disc brakes brought huge doses of stopping power.

1993 Ducati Superlight

Any Ducati is a rare sight on American roads, partly because their assembly process is largely done by hand. But the 900SS SL Superlight will be particularly scarce, as a total of only 300 were imported to the United States

As unique as the Superlight is, the components that are used in its construction are not all that exotic—at least for Ducati. Based on the 900SS SP model, the Superlight is first dressed in a coat of Fly Yellow paint—a radical departure from the traditional Ducati red. Complementing the sporting paint treatment is a solo seat, which dispels any notions of two-up riding.

In the hardware department, the Superlight has a stock 904-cc V-twin decked out in carbon fiber regalia. Almost every nonstructural cover on the engine has been replaced with a carbon fiber version. Even the upswept exhaust canisters are formed in carbon fiber to trim every ounce from the Superlight's fighting weight, which comes in at a feathery 390 pounds.

The 904-cc Pantah V-twin uses a cogged belt to drive the camshafts rather than Ducati's traditional shaft with bevel gears. It also uses a dry clutch as opposed to the usual wet clutch, allowing a drilled cover to be used in order to (you guessed it) save weight. Carbon-fiber front fender and muffler do their part to trim mass. A racing-style fuel cap adds a competition touch. So rare is the Superlight that each example is numbered.

273

1993 Harley-Davidson FLSTN Heritage Softail

Ever since William "Willie G." Davidson, grandson of a Harley-Davidson founder, took over as chief of design in 1963, the company has shown a willingness—a passion even—for bringing daring designs to market. But this one is unusual even by Harley-Davidson standards.

For 1993, Harley offered anniversary models to celebrate the company's 90th birthday, and right alongside those two-tone silver anniversary bikes was this striking black-and-white Heritage Softail with heifer trim, soon to be nicknamed the "Cow Glide." Combining the classic look of wire wheels, whitewall tires, running boards, and chromed headlight nacelle with the black-on-white paint scheme resulted in a classic look. Add the bovine trim, and the image is truly unique.

But like other Harley-Davidson "factory customs," the FLSTN boasts modern mechanicals, such as belt drive, disc brakes, hydraulic forks, and Harley's Softail frame that looks rigid, but isn't. Also like most of its other customs, the Cow Glide sold out immediately, its 2700 copies not near enough to go around.

Plaque below the ignition switch lists the sequence number out of the total production run of just 2700 copies. Bovine trim details the tank top, and is also found on the seat and saddlebags. Chrome fork cover is reminiscent of those found on Harleys of the Fifties.

1993 Harley-Davidson FXDWG Wide Glide

As with previous anniversaries, Harley-Davidson's 90th was celebrated with specially designed and badged models. This time around, it was the Wide Glide that got the treatment.

First introduced in 1980, the Wide Glide featured a flamed "Fat Bob" gas tank, narrow front wheel, "ape hanger" handlebars, forward-mounted foot pegs, bobbed rear fender, and widely spaced fork tubes, from which it got its name. That look carried through to the 90th Anniversary Edition, though a two-tone silver paint scheme replaced the 1980 model's flames.

Beneath the custom styling rests the usual Harley mechanicals, including modern suspension, disc brakes, and of course, the thumping 80-cubic-inch Evolution V-twin. Unlike the original, however, the 90th Anniversary Edition has silent-running, maintenance-free belt drive.

To those familiar with the company's history, the mere presence of a 90th Anniversary Harley-Davidson was a cause for celebration. Several times over the years the Milwaukee company looked as though it was on the verge of extinction, most recently in the early 1980s. But by the time this Wide Glide rolled out the door, Harley-Davidson was in the enviable position of not being able to keep up with orders. No doubt the FXDWG only added to that problem.

1994 BMW R1100RSL

Though BMW had by this time adopted inline three- and four-cylinder engines for its most modern machines, the traditional horizontally opposed "boxer" twin that had long been synonymous with the company's name continued to power some of its most popular models.

That's not to say, however, that the twin hadn't undergone some modernizing of its own. Both the fuel delivery and the three-way, closed-loop catalytic converter were now controlled by an onboard microcomputer that could humble many PCs of the day. Four-valve heads were used, and each of the connecting rods was cracked into two halves around the main boss during production to leave a "unique fracture surface" that provided a perfect alignment upon reassembly.

Front and rear wheels were managed with a suspension system unique to BMW. The Telelever front end consisted of a telescopic fork united with a swingarm that pivoted off the frame and activated a single coil-over shock. The single-sided swingarm housed the drive shaft and was controlled by a gas-filled shock. And complementing the triple discs was an optional anti-lock brake system.

Rider comfort has always been a priority at BMW, and in this, too, the RSL broke new ground. Equipped with adjustable handlebars, hand controls, seat, and windshield, the RSL could be fine-tuned to almost any rider's personal tastes.

R1100RSL retained BMW's traditional "boxer" twin, but it was now fitted with four-valve heads, electronic fuel injection, and catalytic converter. Single-sided swingarm enclosed the drive shaft, and antilock brakes were optional; the toothed "trigger wheels" for the ABS were attached to the inside of the front and rear brake discs. BMW's unique Telelever front suspension used telescopic forks to locate the wheel, but the suspension action itself was controlled by a swingarm attached to the frame at one end and the forks at the other.

1994 Buell S2 Thunderbolt

By combining the latest hardware from Buell with the financial backing of Harley-Davidson, the S2 Thunderbolt was poised to make a full-scale attack on the popular sportbike market.

Eric Buell was certainly no amateur when it came to performance motorcycles, as he had been designing and building Harley-powered sportbikes since the late Eighties. In the past, however, production had rarely exceeded 100 to 120 units per year; with Harley-Davidson newly entrenched as a 49-percent partner, annual sales were expected to number in the thousands.

Harley-Davidson tried marketing its own sports-oriented motorcycle back in 1977 with little success, but that bike, the XLCR, could hardly match the performance of lighter, more powerful Japanese entries. The S2, boasting Buell's latest technical refinements, promised to be a stronger contender.

Powering the S2 was a modified 1203-cc V-twin from the Harley-Davidson Sportster, which rested on rubber mounts to reduce vibration to a more comfortable level. Each of the space-age frames was built by hand from chromoly tubing. Out front was a huge 13-inch brake rotor gripped by a six-piston Brembo caliper, while in back, an aluminum swingarm activated an extension coil-over shock mounted beneath the engine.

The combination of a low center of gravity, sophisticated suspension, and compact 55-inch wheelbase ensured that the Buell S2 Thunderbolt handled like no other Harley-powered bike before it. And the Sportster-based engine ensured that it sounded like no other sportbike on the road.

As did the Harley Sportster from which it garnered its engine, the S2 used a toothed belt to drive the rear wheel instead of a chain. Note the black muffler that dumps its exhaust just ahead of the rear wheel (it's barely visible beneath the left side of the engine); most other sportbikes display their mufflers prominently. Headlight and tail-light are flanked by decorative grilles.

1994 Ducati 916

Late in the 1994 model year, Ducati unleashed a new warrior into the superbike arena. After chalking up numerous victories on racetracks around the world, the 916 set out to make its mark on the street.

Though its engine spotted two cylinders and 100 ccs to most liter-class competitors, the 916 was a serious threat to Japanese rivals. Displacing 916 ccs and boasting an 11:1 compression ratio, Ducati's traditional V-twin with unique desmodromic valve actuation pumped 105 horsepower to the rear wheel. While that hardly made the 916 the most powerful bike in its class, a combination of composite materials, compact design, and weight-saving engineering certainly made it one of the lightest; at 438 pounds, the 916 could best be described as svelte.

Since just 400 were planned to be exported to the United States, the 916 became an instant collectible. But those fortunate enough to snare one were also rewarded with a graceful and exotic expression of a state-of-the-art superbike—Italian style.

The 916 broke with Ducati tradition in having its V-twin water cooled, but carried the company's unique desmodromic valvetrain along with four-valve heads and fuel injection. Exhaust is routed through mufflers mounted beneath the tail fairing. Copper-colored cylinder behind the fork brace is a steering stabilizer that helps reduce the "twitchiness" that results from a short wheelbase and steep fork angle.

1994 Harley-Davidson FLHTC Electra-Glide

In motorcycle parlance, the Harley-Davidson FLHTC represents what's known as a "full dresser," being equipped with luxuries riders of 30 years ago never even envisioned.

It wasn't until the 1940s that windshields became common, the military being among the first to use them—with the hope of stopping more than just wind from going through the rider's hair. Later in the decade, Harley-Davidson offered a roll-up windshield as an option on civilian bikes.

In those days, riders felt lucky to get instruments and warning lights on their mounts. As might be expected, motorcycling has come a long way since then. The FLHTC Ultra Classic Electra-Glide features air-adjustable suspension, quiet belt-drive, an electronic cruise control, CB radio, AM/FM amplified stereo with weather band that includes remote controls for the passenger, a spacious rear trunk, and heavily-padded seats with backrests, all of which make its passengers feel right at home— even when they're miles away.

In the old days, riders probably never dreamed that touring could be so luxurious. Nowadays, they don't have to.

There's storage space aplenty on the FLHTC, including compartments in the lower fairing. Eighty-cubic-inch Evolution V-twin introduced in 1984 provides sufficient power to motivate the dresser's 765 pounds. Cushy passenger's throne is flanked by speakers for the stereo; they have their own volume control as well. Script on the front fender says a mouthful.

1995 Harley-Davidson FXSTSB Bad Boy

When is a bad boy good? When it's a Harley custom, that's when.

Introduced in 1995, the Bad Boy was based on the company's Softail Springer model, but was cloaked in black from its narrow front fender to its bobbed tail. Even such traditionally bright pieces as the fork tubes, instrument panel, and under-seat oil tank were blacked out. Only the front coil springs, headlight, exhaust pipes, handlebars, and various trim pieces carried chrome.

Though the look was retro, the technology was up to date. Springer front forks, similar in concept to those used on Harleys up through the Forties, had arrived in 1988 carrying an updated design, and on the Bad Boy, also incorporated a multi-link arrangement that allowed the fender to hug the 21-inch tire more closely. The frame that looked rigid wasn't, as it was Harley's Softail design that incorporated a swingarm extending two shocks underneath the engine. Power came from the company's 80-cubic-inch Evolution V-twin, and drilled disc brakes were featured front and back. The slotted rear wheel was turned by a toothed belt instead of a chain, same as other Harleys of the period.

Despite its appeal, the Bad Boy led a short life. Production lasted only three years, during which

time little changed besides the tank striping, which was available in yellow, blue, and red.

Tank-mounted instrument panel and handlebar risers, usually finished in chrome, were black on the Bad Boy. Special to this model was an enameled tank badge reminiscent of a piece of jewelry. Surrounding stripes came in yellow, blue, or red. Slotted cast rear wheel was driven by toothed belt per Harley practice of the day. Chrome spring and shock highlight the black springer forks.

1996 Aprilia RS250

Aprilia arrived on the motorcycle scene only recently, but has already made a big splash in Europe.

Starting as a small bicycle manufacturer, the Italian company did not build its first motorcycles until the mid Seventies. The first examples were mopeds, quickly followed by small trail bikes. All used proprietary engines made by outside manufacturers, a philosophy that continues at Aprilia today.

Some of the company's racing bikes were powered by engines built in-house, but most carried proprietary units. One of the latter, fitted with a Rotax engine, proved fairly successful in the late Eighties, and capitalizing on its victories put Aprilia's 125- and 250-cc road bikes in the limelight.

Though scooters and mopeds contributed mightily to Aprilia's meteoric rise during the Nineties, its RS250 sportbike was what really made the company take off. Powered by a highly tuned version of a Suzuki two-stroke V-twin, it was essentially a road racer for the street, and proved very popular.

Aprilia has since grown into one of Europe's largest motorcycle producers, one of its more notable efforts being the Pegaso 650. Combining a trail bike's suspension and large single-cylinder engine with sportbike styling, the Pegaso was a huge hit, prompting a whole new class of bikes in Europe.

Intended to commemorate—and capitalize upon—Aprilia's 1994 World Championship title, the RS250 was a raving success in Europe. A tank decal announces the victory. Odd-looking expansion chambers for the two-stroke V-twin culminate in carbon-fiber mufflers. Many of the chassis's components, like the swingarm, combine art with function.

1996 Boss Hoss

No question about it, this is the biggest, baddest motorcycle that ever roamed the streets. And lest it be discounted as some kind of one-off custom-built absurdity, rest assured the Boss Hoss is a production vehicle—though production is admittedly limited.

At the heart of what is perhaps the ultimate expression of the "bigger is better" philosophy is a Chevy V-8. Most, such as the example pictured, use the venerable small-block variant of 350 cubic inches—that's 5700 ccs— but newer versions are available with a big-block V-8 of 502 cubic inches. Horsepower output ranges from 355 for the base small-block to 502 for the hottest big-block.

Yes, of course that's absurd.

Boss Hoss was founded in 1990 by Monte Warne, who decided to begin selling copies of his outrageous V-8 motorcycle after it drew crowds—and numerous potential buyers—at that year's Daytona Speedweek celebration. Approximately 1750 have rolled out of the Dyersburg, Tennessee, factory since then, though production is now up to about 500 per year. Recently, V-6 versions (with "only" 200 horsepower) have been added to the roster, as have three-wheeled trikes.

Early versions had a one-speed transmission with hand-operated, vacuum-assisted clutch, but the clutch was later replaced by a torque converter, and current machines get a two-speed automatic. None are light on the road—or on the wallet: A small-block V-8 version of the seven-foot-long motorcycle tips the scales at 1100 pounds and starts at around $28,000, while a big-block adds 200 pounds and $7000 to those figures.

But such is the price to be King.

Huge, triple disc brakes that nearly hide the wheels behind them are reassuring. Massively wide, nine-gallon fuel tank houses a complete set of gauges. Rear tire is from a car; taillight gives away the Boss's secret.

1997 Ducati 750 Monster

While a swoopy, full-coverage fairing was a defining necessity for any self-respecting sportbike of the Nineties, a new breed of performance machine was beginning to bloom. Stripped of all non-essentials, bikes like Ducati's Monster were starting a new trend toward minimalist motorcycles.

On the Monster, there's nothing to shroud the tubular trellis frame or V-twin engine. As opposed to Ducati's race-inspired sportbikes that carried exotic four-valve, water-cooled V-twins, the Monster came with a less-sophisticated air-cooled, two-valve engine, though it still sported the company's signature desmodromic valve actuation. The machine's simplistic nature meant even a tachometer was superfluous, but the approach resulted in a feather-light curb weight of just 390 pounds.

As a result, the Monster followed a formula that proved so successful with American muscle cars of the Sixties: light weight, powerful engine, basic amenities, low price. Introduced in 1993 with a 900-cc V-twin, smaller 750- and 600-cc Monsters followed, though the last wasn't sold in the United States until recently.

The back-to-basics Monster started life with an air-cooled, two-valve, 900-cc V-twin, but smaller, less-expensive versions followed; this 750 was the entry-level model in the United States. No-nonsense philosophy deemed a tachometer unnecessary, but there was no skimping on brake hardware: Big Brembo floating discs were used, though there was only one on the front wheel rather than the pair that appeared on most sporting Ducatis.

1997 Harley-Davidson FLSTF Fat Boy

Since its introduction in 1990, the Fat Boy has remained one of Harley-Davidson's most popular models. Over the next decade, waiting lists for the machines sometimes stretched as long as two years.

The original Fat Boy came in any color you wanted—as long as you wanted grey. Fenders, fuel tank, oil tank, and even the frame were all painted the same hue, with fine yellow trim being applied around the valve covers, ignition switch, primary-cover inspection plate, timing cover, and within the winged tank emblem. But the most noticeable element of the Fat Boy's styling

were the 16-inch solid wheels used both front and rear; it remains, to this day, the only model so equipped.

Fat Boys rode the Softail frame

that hid its shocks beneath the engine. Power came from the 80-cubic-inch Evolution V-twin introduced six years earlier, and like all Harleys since, used belt drive.

After 1990, Fat Boys were available in a variety of colors, including two-tones—though grey was never again offered. Otherwise, however, they changed little until a redesigned model sporting Harley's new Twin Cam 88 V-twin arrived in 2000. Yet the company knew to leave well enough alone, and today's Fat Boy is nearly indistinguishable from the original.

Except for that grey paint….

Solid wheels front and rear distinguish the Fat Boy from other models in the line. Note svelte fenders with ducktail trailing edges. Headlight treatment dates from 1949, and is used on several current Harleys. Power comes from an 80-cubic-inch Evolution complete with monogrammed air cleaner.

1997 Harley-Davidson FXSTS Heritage Springer

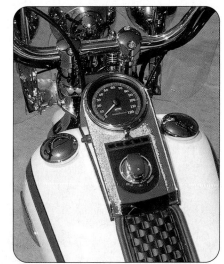

Nicknamed the "Old Boy" by Harley-Davidson upon its introduction in 1997, the FXSTS was initially available only in white with either red or blue trim. Black was the standard color in '98, though maroon-and-gold 95th Anniversary editions were also offered; since then, other colors have been added.

As the name suggests, this model was designed to look like Harley-Davidsons of years passed. Though "retro" styling was certainly nothing new to the company, this model looked further back than the others: specifically, to the 1940s.

The front fender design dated from before World War II, as did the fender light. Forties-style springer forks had been reincarnated by Harley-Davidson in the late Eighties, but up to now had been used only on custom models. Tank badges mimicked those from '40 to '46, and the fringed saddlebags and "tombstone" taillight were in use during the same period.

Otherwise, the Old Boy enjoyed the modern mechanicals of the other Harley Big Twins, including front and rear disc brakes, 80-cubic-inch Evolution V-twin, and belt drive.

1997 Ural

If the Russian-built Ural looks markedly similar to an old BMW, that's only because it is.

After World War II, Russia seized BMW's plant in Germany and moved the tooling and equipment back to the Soviet Union. A short time later, what were essentially reproductions based on parts from different BMW models hit the market carrying Ural badges.

Though the design has seen updates over the years, today's models still closely resemble the originals—and, by association, more modern BMWs. The 650-cc horizontally opposed twin remains a simple overhead-valve affair, and sidecar versions retain the option of having a powered wheel that comes in handy on rough terrain. Suspension is by traditional swingarm with coil-over shocks in back, but in front is a modified Earles fork reminiscent of those used on BMWs from the mid Fifties to the late Sixties. Wheels retain drum brakes and are interchangeable; the spare can be fitted to any of the three corners.

Though it looks ungainly and crude in today's light, a Ural with sidecar can be purchased for about $6000—quite a transportation bargain. And the fact that the 60-year-old design is still in production is also an off-hand compliment to its original German maker.

Though the sleek fairing would look to be more at home on an Eighties sportbike, other components of the Ural appear more antiquated and pedestrian. The 650-cc, overhead-valve, horizontally opposed twin puts out about 35 horsepower, and with the exception of more modern carburetion, closely resembles a BMW engine—of 60 years ago. Earles-type forks are also reminiscent of BMWs of long ago, as is the powered sidecar wheel. No, the speedometer isn't wildly optimistic; it's calibrated in kilometers per hour, not miles per hour.

1997 Yamaha Royal Star Palamino Edition

Yamaha's latest interpretation of the cruiser concept differs from that of most other manufacturers, particularly in the engine department. Whereas the traditional formula calls for a 45-degree V-twin, this Japanese company chose a different route.

First of all, it's not a V-twin at all, but rather a V-four. Cylinder banks of the 1300-cc engine are separated by 70 degrees, and each is topped with double-overhead cams. Though the cylinders have fins cast into them, the engine is primarily water cooled. And final drive is by shaft.

Elsewhere the Royal Star is perhaps more con-ventional, though the unusual cast spoke wheels are almost completely hidden by the large brake discs. But what really sets this special edition apart are the fine details.

Cream opalescent paint is accented with tan imitation leather on the seat, saddlebags, and tank strap, all of which are also studded. Even the hand grips are covered in matching material, and chrome trim abounds.

With its early-Eighties Virago, Yamaha was the first Japanese company to hit the market with a cruiser-style bike. Perhaps the Royal Star will lead the concept into the 21st Century.

Though it looks like a wide-angle, air-cooled V-twin, the Royal Star sports a water-cooled V-four. Large brake discs hide seven-spoke cast wheels. Faux leather trim graces the hand grips and tank strap, while the tank itself boasts fine striping detail.

1998 Bimota SB6 R

During the 1990s, one of Bimota's strongest sellers was the SB6, powered by a Suzuki GSXR1100 four-cylinder engine. (In Bimota-speak, the first letter of the model designation is the first initial of the engine supplier.) But as the decade drew to a close, the venerable SB6 evolved into the even higher-tech SB6 R.

Introduced in 1998, the bike shown is the first SB6 R off the production line. "Straight Connection Technology" is Bimota's term for the massive aluminum-alloy structure that connects the front forks and rear swingarm pivot. Fully adjustable Paioli upside-down forks hold a pair of floating rotors squeezed by Brembo calipers. Power is still supplied by a 1074-cc Suzuki four.

Joining the exotic aluminum frame in the battle against unwanted weight are numerous carbon-fiber components, including the fenders and several pieces of non-structural bodywork. Still, the Bimota only weighs about 20-30 pounds less than a comparable Suzuki—and costs well over twice as much. But exclusivity doesn't come without cost.

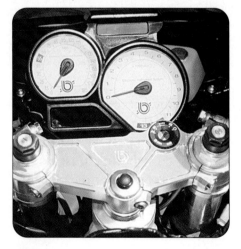

Aluminum alloy and carbon fiber join forces to trim weight from the SB6 R. Power comes from a 1074-cc Suzuki GSXR1100 water-cooled four, redlined at an energetic 11,500 rpm. The combination of light weight and prodigious output resulted in a sportbike of extraordinary capabilities.

1998 Ducati ST2

In somewhat of a departure for Ducati, the ST2 of 1998 was aimed squarely at the sport-touring crowd. Yet despite its more relaxed driving position and touring amenities, the ST2 still boasted the kind of performance expected of the marque.

Along with an analog speedometer and tach, the ST2 includes a digital display for fuel level, engine temperature, and time of day. Rearview mirrors are spring-loaded to help absorb shock, and the full-coverage fairing offers the driver an increased level of protection from the elements. Integrated saddlebags can swallow a full-face helmet and are detachable with the turn of a key, while the sleek 5.5-gallon fuel tank allows plenty of pleasurable miles between stops.

But Ducati didn't forget the "sport" in "sport-touring." Along with triple Brembo floating disc brakes, the ST2 featured fully adjustable suspension and a powerful 904-cc, water-cooled, fuel-injected V-twin with Ducati's famous desmodromic valvetrain. Though this was a two-valve version of the V-twin, a four-valve variant appeared shortly thereafter carrying the ST4 designation.

Sculpted fuel tank holds a full 5.5 gallons, and combined with the full-coverage fairing with integrated turn signals, encourages long-distance touring. The ST2's "handlebars" aren't so much bars as artful castings bolted to the tops of the fork tubes.

1998 Harley-Davidson FLHRCI Road King Classic

I n celebration of Harley-Davidson's 95th anniversary, the company released special editions of its motorcycles with a maroon and gold paint scheme along with special 95th-anniversary emblems. Not all 1998 models received the treatment; the 95th package was listed as a factory option.

Combining classic styling with standard saddlebags and detachable windshield, the Road King has been one of Harley-Davidson's most popular models since its introduction in the mid Nineties. Power initially came from the 80-cubic-inch Evolution V-twin, with the new Twin Cam 88 taking its place for 1999.

By 1998, the Road King was being offered in two versions: base and Classic. Differentiating the latter were hard bags covered in leather (the base had regular hard bags), whitewall tires, distinct badging, and slanted exhaust tips. Classics also got standard fuel injection (contributing the "I" in the model designation), which was optional on the base model. Shown here is a Classic dressed in 95th-anniversary attire.

The 80-cubic-inch (1340-cc) Evo V-twin wore a monogrammed air cleaner. Never at a loss for brightwork, this Road King sports its classic Harley headlight nacelle in chrome.

1998 Honda Valkyrie

As Japanese manufacturers rushed to bring out cruiser models in the 1980s, Honda was in the thick of things with its V-twin Shadows. During the Nineties, these cruisers grew in displacement and sophistication, but Honda trumped them all with the 1997 introduction of the Valkyrie.

Unlike the typical V-twins and occasional V-four, the Valkyrie was powered by the flat six used in Honda's big Gold Wing tourer. Displacing 1520 ccs, it sported individual carbs for each cylinder. Since it lacked the extensive bodywork of the Gold Wing, the gleaming chrome-plated engine took center stage on this seven-foot-long motorcycle.

Like the Gold Wing, the Valkyrie had shaft drive, and its triple disc brakes provided plenty of stopping power. The six-cylinder engine was much smoother in operation than competing V-twins, and though that feature veered it away from traditional cruiser styling, it could outpower anything in its class.

Unlike most rivals, which mounted their instruments on the tank, the Valkyrie carried them in bullet-shaped pods above the headlight.

Chrome-encrusted 1520-cc flat six provided power and smoothness previously unknown in the cruiser class.

1998 Triumph T595

Triumph made a resurgence in the 1990s, though it was admittedly in name only; the original company was long gone by that time, as was the fabled factory at Meridan.

Credited with the return was John Bloor, who had put up the money to fund a range of completely new motorcycles that was six years in the making. They were powered by water-cooled triples and fours displacing 750 to 1200 ccs, and included standard, sport, touring, and eventually dual-purpose models.

The most sporting of the new Triumphs were the 750-cc three-cylinder and 1000-cc four-cylinder Daytonas. Wrapped in sleek bodywork, they were powerful enough, but taller and heavier than their Japanese rivals. That all changed in 1997.

With the introduction of the T595 that year, Triumph was back in the game. This revised Daytona sported a 955-cc fuel-injected triple in a new alloy frame, and the combination proved potent. And though the Triumph name was perhaps more closely associated with "standard" models, the T595 quickly became the marque's best-seller.

Sleek bodywork of the T595 combined with a strong 955-cc, water-cooled, fuel-injected triple to produce a competitive sporting mount. These new Triumphs had little association with the Triumphs of old, as about the only thing carried over was the stylized logo—and even that was changed some.

1998 Triumph Thunderbird Sport

Among the array of models offered by the "New Triumph" was the semi-sport Thunderbird. Wearing little more than a bikini fairing and streamlined tailpiece, it bridged the gap between the sleek Daytona sportbike and the "standard" Trident.

Bearing a name resurrected from Triumph models of the Fifties, the Thunderbird carried many styling elements from the company's past life. The shape, lettering, and striping of the fuel tank mimicked those from the Seventies, and the air cleaner and side covers also looked like those found on Triumphs of old.

Side covers wear a badge along with the traditional Union Jack flag. Twin-cam, water-cooled triple displaced 885-ccs, its three exhaust pipes flowing into two mufflers; the two outside pipes joined together under the engine. Fuel tank resembled Triumphs of old, both in shape and trim.

On the mechanical side, however, it was a different story. While a three-cylinder engine was also used in the Trident of the Seventies, the one powering the Thunderbird was larger (885 ccs versus 750), water-cooled rather than air-cooled (though it still sported "fins"), and was of modern double-over-head-cam design rather than the old overhead-valve layout. Spoked wheels held dual 12-inch disc brakes in front, a single 11-inch disc in the rear—braking power the old Triumphs could only dream of.

2000 MV Agusta F4 Strada

Twenty years after the last production model rolled off the assembly line, MV Agusta made a comeback. Or at least the name did.

Always expensive and thus exclusive, MV built its reputation with road bikes that closely resembled the company's legendary racing machines. But by the late 1970s, those bikes that were expensive to buy proved even more expensive to build,

and the company ceased operations in 1980.

But in 1991, the MV Agusta name was purchased by Cagiva, an up-and-coming Italian motorcycle manufacturer that already owned Ducati. Soon Cagiva was having financial troubles of its own, however, and it wasn't until 1997 that the revered name once again graced a fuel tank.

It was worth the wait. The initial versions, called F4 Oro, were

powered by a 750-cc, four-cylinder, fuel-injected engine and constructed of exotic, lightweight materials. Only about 200 were built—at around $32,000 apiece. They were followed by regular production F4s (called Strada) that looked nearly the same but sold for a much more reasonable $19,000. At last count, demand far exceeded supply, and MV Agusta once again became a name to be reckoned with.

Though lacking some of the exotic materials that made up the $32,000 limited-edition Oro versions, the F4 Strada continued the MV Agusta tradition of excellence at a price—in this case, a still-lofty $19,000. At 445 pounds, the Strada was a lightweight for the 750 class, but the Oro, boasting magnesium castings and carbon-fiber bodywork, cut about 20 pounds from that figure—meaning the diet cost nearly $700 a pound. MV Agusta decal followed the design of those used on the last of the "originals" in the late Seventies; note the turn signals integrated into the rearview mirrors. A quartet of exhaust pipes exits from beneath the tailpiece.

Index